the mind-bod
internet guide

1 50
£4
2002

the mind-body-spirit internet guide

Compiled by // **Gerry Maguire Thompson**

Thorsons

To Sadie Thompson 1913–2000,
who never once surfed the Net.

Thorsons
An Imprint of HarperCollins*Publishers*
77–85 Fulham Palace Road
Hammersmith, London W6 8JB

The Thorsons website address is: www.thorsons.com

First published 2001

10 9 8 7 6 5 4 3 2 1

© Gerry Maguire Thompson, 2001

Gerry Maguire Thompson asserts the moral right to be
identified as the author of this work

A catalogue record of this book is
available from the British Library

ISBN 0 00 710641 6

Printed and bound in Great Britain by
Martins The Printers Ltd, Berwick Upon Tweed

acknowledgements

Special thanks for invaluable research assistance to Tim Norman, a website designer whom you can contact at timnorman@beeb.net.

Thanks also to Sarah Litvinoff, Paul Levy, Emma Amyatt-Leir, Elaine Bellamy and to all at Thorsons, especially Louise McNamara and Paul Redhead.

Nowadays people can change the world without leaving their computers.

frontispiece

This book covers the whole mind-body-spirit field and contains almost a thousand websites and other Internet resources. Websites on the Internet come and go, but this book will give you strategies that will enable you to find what you want despite the changes. It also explains comprehensively how to surf the Net, and how to go about other Internet activities such as email, discussion groups, online chat and shopping.

contents

MIND 133

SPIRIT

introduction

The Mind-Body-Spirit Internet Guide offers you access to a vast wealth of fascinating transformative material that can be found online today. It covers everything in the field from Atlantis, Bioenergetics and Colonics, to Wicca, Yoga and Zen. It opens up just about every major form of religion, spiritual path, mysticism, consciousness, ecology, therapy and oracular device. It mingles the newest, coolest buzzwords with the most ancient and timeless of wisdom.

Enlightenment is only a mouse-click away. The world is changing very very fast. Gone are the days when the only way to find out about aromatherapy or Zoroastrianism was to go out and buy a book. Today, it's easier, cheaper and more convenient to get on the Net. And this is the future – as time passes, this is going to be more and more so. Even if you do want to get the book – or locate a local class to study the subject – searching on the Net is still going to be the easiest way to find it.

No-one can afford to ignore the Net any longer. The Net is going to make a big difference to the way we live our lives – and not least to those who are interested in matters of mind-body-spirit. For many of us, it's making a difference already. For the rest, the differences are going to filter down through to us quicker than we'd ever think possible. That's the way these things work.

The trick, though, is in finding what you are looking for when accessing the Internet. To start with, there's so much stuff out there. So the crucial question is how you conduct your search. And by the way, in the time that's passed since you started reading the previous sentence, there's a whole lot more stuff out there. So you need some methods and strategies to deal with it all. This book will give you those. So even as websites come and go these tools and techniques will still serve you well. Particular search strategies to help you in an environment where sites come and go are set out on page 64.

In cyberspace, nobody can hear you scream 'quality control!'

Secondly, a whole lot of that stuff – by far the greater part of it – is not going to be what you want. Maybe it's not about the precise subject you had in mind, or doesn't cover the exact aspect you were looking for. Maybe it doesn't adopt the right approach, or doesn't suit your taste. Or most likely of all, maybe it's just crap; there's a lot of useless stuff out there. Nobody is monitoring the quality; anybody can upload anything they like onto the Net, anywhere they wish, anytime they want.

Learning the lingo

In the course of your perambulations round the Net, you'll encounter a lot of technical terms, jargon and slang. Most of these will seem obscure and inexplicable, if not downright bizarre. This linguistic phenomenon has come about because of the influence of those enthusiasts who have pioneered the Internet, earning the privilege of setting its language fashions. These leading lights have mainly been computer technicians, west coast hipsters, valley girls, geeks, nerds and other people who really should get out more. And their language is sticking. That's why you'll need to pick up some basic esoteric vocabulary such as cookies, spam, lurkers, hotspots, flame wars, emoticons and FAQs. You'll find all these terms explained as they crop up in the text; or you can look them up right now if you want in the glossary at the back of the book on page 289. When one of these terms is introduced for the first time, you'll see it highlighted in **bold**. For instance, **e-lying** – exaggerating the number of **hits** your website is getting, to impress your girlfriend/boss/ potential venture capital investors. **Cyberflirtation** and

cyberchondria are now official dictionary **e-words**, as are **pagejacking** and **cybersquatter**. Also **yetties** – youthful entrepreneurs who make their fortune from the Internet. Less official but still universally recognized in webspeak are terms such as **boboru** – Burned Out, But Optimistic (for Reasons Unknown). The abbreviation for 'Members Of The Opposite Sex' **motos**, favoured by email correspondents, appears to have been replaced by the more politically correct **motas** (member of the appropriate sex).

About this book

We hope you will find this guide informative and comprehensive, accessible and user-friendly, lively and entertaining. While focusing mainly on the most serious and substantial information, we have still found room for the Internet's other fare – the fun stuff, the tongue-in-cheek, the trivial and off-the-wall or off-the-planet offerings. They're probably not going to leave you any the wiser, but they do form a significant element of the Internet and so deserve to be represented, and they can be fun.

As much a guide as a directory, this book will steer you through a vast labyrinth of Internet resources, revealing how to navigate effectively and avoid pitfalls. It shows you how and where to find the kind of information you're looking for, and it gives you tips on how to find the gems among the rubbish. It offers strategies to deal with the fast-changing nature of the Net. As well as giving the low-down on particular sources, it equips you with the means to embark on your own journeys of discovery of brand-new material.

With this book, you will be able to:

- get information about almost any mind-body-spirit subject;
- locate and buy products and services;
- find teachers, courses and centres;
- make friends and connect with kindred spirits;
- obtain news or advice and join discussions in your chosen areas of interest;
- and do lots of other things that I can't think of right now.

Mind-body-spirit websites can be ephemeral. Because these sites are usually run by small groups or individuals rather than large corporations, their maintenance may be erratic. They may well switch servers or change addresses without notice. If you have trouble accessing any of the sites listed in this book, try typing in the address into your favourite search engine – very often it will track down sites for you that appear to have gone AWOL.

If you find something has vanished, or if you come across any sites that you think should be in the next edition of the guide, you're most welcome to email me the address and brief comments at **gerry@pavilion.co.uk.**

1 the Internet – past, present and future

We're living in a very exciting time. Our methods of communication with one another are going through the fastest period of change ever. And it's mainly because of the sudden and dramatic entry into our lives of the phenomenon known as the Internet.

The Net is a very loose conglomeration of computers and connections between them. It has a number of areas, the most important of which from our point of view are the **World Wide Web** (or **www**) and **Usenet**. The www is that part of the Net which is made with **HTML** (hyper text markup language). This is where you do your **surfing**, or navigating round the material there looking for stuff.

The Net began to take shape in the Cold War 1960s, as a closed military link-up of computers and control centres for defence purposes. Then educational and research establishments became part of the network for information exchange, and gradually other forms of organization came on board. Finally, individuals were able to hook up, and the basis of the Web as we know it today was born.

The Net has been created mainly through the connections already offered by telephone lines. Each computer terminal on the network is connected to the phone network through a **modem** which converts the computer data into signals that can be handled by that network. Most private Net users connect through an **Internet Service Provider** or **ISP** to plug into the main channels or **spines** of the Web. The user can go **online** or **log on** at any time by using computer software to dial up the ISP and establish a connection through their **server**. Before going online for the first time, you will need to **configure** your connection software with your own Internet Protocol (IP) address, and details of the ISP's server, phone number and so on. ISPs will usually help with this through their **helplines**; most provide software on a CD which will configure your browser for you.

Getting connected: choosing an Internet Service Provider (ISP)

Like just about everything else on the Net, the ways that ISPs offer their services are in a state of rapid flux. These days most of them offer a free service where you only pay for the connecting phone calls at local rates. They obtain their revenue by paying less for this phone time than you would, and pocketing the difference. Some ISPs now also offer some free phone time (an **unmetered connection**) as well, usually in the evenings and at weekends. But other ISPs still charge a modest monthly or yearly fee; this can sometimes still be a good deal because you usually get a free, high quality help service and can often get online more quickly. Some of the bigger ISPs, such as AOL and Compuserve, also offer their own organized website **content** and other information provision as well as providing a connection service. This is called becoming a **portal**. For an up-to-date list of ISPs of different kinds and assessment of their services it's best to consult a local Internet magazine.

Once you're online, you can begin to send **email** or search the Web for websites that are of interest to you. Or you might want to get news, join a discussion group or **chat** room with kindred spirits, or do some online shopping. All these activities are described in detail in their respective chapters that follow.

Accessing the Web

You can use a number of different devices to access the Web. The most commonly used is still the regular computer, though this may change soon. There are three main types of computer from which to choose, each with a different **operating system** or **OS**.

- Personal Computers or PCs use the Microsoft **Windows** operating system, sometimes called **Wintel** because it has traditionally used Intel microprocessors or **chips**. Most computers these days use this system, so there are advantages in terms of software availability and compatibility. However, there are inherent weaknesses in this OS, because it has been built up in successive layers of programming that still include coding from the original **DOS** system. This can lead to computer crashes as well as vulnerability to hacking and viruses (see page 59). Windows OSs include Windows 95, 98, 2000 and Millennium Edition (Me for short).
- The Apple Macintosh range of computers uses its own operating system; versions that are currently in use range from OS6 to OS9 and the new OSX. The Mac system invented windows, and was the model for Microsoft's developments. It's a cleaner system that crashes less often and is easier to fix when it does. It's altogether a more understandable, user friendly and intuitive set-up, but sometimes creates compatibility problems because it is not the dominant system. Macintosh was doing badly in the market place until the revolutionary Imac revived its fortunes in the late 1990s. Even the most ancient Macs run windows and last for ever, and so can be good for beginners who want to get the hang of computers.
- The Linux operating system is at present mainly espoused by computer programming freaks but may be a threat to Windows domination in the future.

In the last year or two, other options for accessing the Net have appeared, with a special emphasis on getting online while away from your home or desk. Most prominent among these at present is the **WAP** (Wireless Application Protocol) telephones. These can be used for sending email and viewing simple websites that have been specially created for their use. They have a small screen and use the number pads to key in text. Although large corporations have invested heavily in their development, no-one is quite sure at this moment whether they're becoming the next big thing or are just about to be superseded by other systems currently in development.

Palm-top computers could be one of those 'other systems'. These are presently able to send email and do surfing if you don't mind them being a bit slow. Their speed is likely to improve radically in the near future.

Some gaming computers such as Amiga Dreamcast and Playstation can be used online, but are also slow at present. This too is likely to change rapidly. Internet access through your TV is also becoming a cheap alternative.

Here's a summary of the main items of software that are used in your computer for Internet access:

- **Dialler** – a program that calls your ISP, uses your password and account details and establishes a connection.
- **Browser** – the tool which enables you to navigate your way round the Web once you're connected.
- **Email program** – for sending electronic mail; sometimes this is built into the browser.
- **Newsgroup reader** – guess what, it's for reading stuff from newsgroups.
- **Virus checking software** (see page 61 for further information on this).
- **Decompression** software – programs for **unzipping** or opening files that have been compressed so that they'll travel faster across Internet connections.
- Other software for coding and decoding web files in a variety of formats such as sound, animation or multimedia.

Use of these different programs is dealt with in following sections of the book.

How stuff is arranged on the Web

- Material on the Web is arranged into **sites**, each of which consists of one or more **pages**.
- The page that you see first on any site is known as the **home page**.
- Sites are found by means of their web **address** or **URL** (Universal Resource Locator).

- These addresses can also appear on other pages throughout the Web, and are then known as **links**. These enable you to go straight to their site or page. Links thus enable sites to be connected one with another, or to be directly accessed from **search tools**.
- Groups of websites can also be arranged into **webrings** that relate to a common subject area. For instance, in the mind-body-spirit field there are webrings that cover everything from astral sex to zen teabags. Many of these are listed in the directory section of this book under their respective subject headings.

Guidance on how to access these resources is given in the section on searching (see page 44).

How the Internet is developing

Lots of people knew the Net was coming, and that it would have an impact on how we live, but few anticipated the speed of it all. In a very short time it has gone from an obscure pursuit of the avant garde to an everyday reality for the person in the street. Businesses are now falling over themselves to have a **web presence** and do **e-commerce**. Other companies that exist purely for online operation are springing up – the dot.com businesses – floating themselves on the stock market, and attracting huge investment. Sometimes it all gets a bit too unrealistic and the bubble seems to be bursting; some companies have been spending almost $1 million dollars a day and not earning any profit. But the trend is still going strong. Other conventional corporations are now desperate to merge with e-businesses, bringing cross-media mega-mergers on a whole new scale. Time-Warner hooked up with AOL (America On Line) to form the world's biggest media company. Phone giant Vodaphone and TV/Internet firm Vivendi have hatched a web presence called Vizzavi, which they are planning to launch to an existing customer base of 70 million people across Europe.

Development of the Net to date has been based on open source technologies that everyone can adopt as standard, but Microsoft and other companies want everyone to adopt technologies which they own, and can therefore control and profit from. The Microsoft company developed a disk operating system (DOS) for PCs, and grew to be by far the strongest influence on software development and computer usage. It was ordered by a US judge to split itself into two separate companies, one to develop its Windows program and one to concentrate on its other software applications. This ruling – still subject to appeal – resulted from alleged anti-competitive practices. Microsoft was accused of abusing its dominant market position, for example, by getting its browser shipped with all PCs. Microsoft would also be obliged to publicly disclose its source code for the Windows Operating System – the secrets of its inner workings. This gigantic lawsuit has been running since the early 1990s. In 1994, Microsoft agreed that they would not require computer makers that license its Windows OS to also license its Internet software. In 1997, they were fined $1 million a day for allegedly violating this agreement. In 1999, the courts found that Microsoft has monopoly power in PC operating systems and that it has used it to harm consumers, computer makers and others. The European Community has recently brought similar legal proceedings against Microsoft.

Sun Microsystems have accused Microsoft of trying to turn Sun's Java computer language, developed as an Internet open standard, into a Microsoft controlled technology. This whole subject is a key issue for the future of the Internet, and the outcomes will influence all our lives in ways that we can't possibly know now. For instance, Microsoft is about to embark on a huge new three-year project, called Next Generation Windows Services, with a budget similar to NASA's moon shot. Bill Gates claims this will usher in 'a new Internet era'; one shudders to think what that might mean. Sounds like a good cue for some positive affirmations.

There is nonetheless an incredibly vibrant feeling of new possibility in the business world as a result of Internet development. Companies and individuals are rushing into all kinds of new ventures, without any way of knowing what the outcomes are going to be. As John Perry Barlow, lyricist of the Grateful Dead, put it: 'The Internet is like the Wild West during the gold rush'. Except, of course, that this time it's everywhere, not just in the West.

Some things to worry about

Microsoft's approach is typical of a trend among software manufacturers, who are increasingly seeking to create products that will get you to do things the way they want you to. The whole concept of a clear distinction between the contents of your computer and what is 'out there' on the Net is breaking down; software is becoming increasingly invasive and restrictive. To take one example, Angus Kennedy – author of the best-selling *Rough Guide to the Internet* – has spoken in interview of AOL's software being 'almost like a virus that takes over your computer'. 'Just don't use it!' he says.

Security is another big area of concern, and **hacking** has been making big news. This is where a skilled computer programmer can gain unauthorized access to the workings of a corporate or governmental computer resource and website, and change things around. Some of the most celebrated recent examples have involved **denial of service** attacks, which leave would-be customers unable to use the sites. A series of these has taken place on such high-profile sites as

Microsoft, Yahoo, Amazon, Buy, CNN and web auctioneers eBay. Companies can incur major financial loss as well as irreparable damage to reputation as a result of such hack-attacks and their attendant publicity. Ebay, for example, lost 26 percent of its market value in five days as a result of a single incident. Serbian cyber-vandals managed to falsely register themselves as owners of a whole host of websites that included Manchester United soccer team, Adidas, Viagra, the James Bond site, and even France and Italy. A total loss of service occurred for a time at the original sites, so that visitors saw instead a page that said 'Kosovo is Serbia'.

Hacking, though, is not a new phenomenon. In 1878, two years after Alexander Graham Bell invented the telephone, teenagers were making prank calls. And in those days, two years was not a long time for innovations.

Internet fraud is on the increase, too. Bill Gates reportedly had his credit card details stolen by a teenage hacker. A 19-year-old Russian hacker called Maxim posted 25,000 stolen card numbers on the Web. In England, visitors to British Telecom's site found that they could access customers' names, addresses, telephone numbers and email addresses. This last incident, and many others like it, were put down to 'human error'. Still worrying, though. Thirty-five percent of US companies reported attacks on their e-commerce sites during the last year.

Then there are the viruses, such as the notorious Love Bug, which swept through computers all over the world in early 2000. For more on viruses, see page 59. Furthermore, material on the Net is of highly variable quality. Unsolicited and extreme pornography is also frequently encountered. All this is a reflection of the fact that the Net is, currently at least, almost completely unregulated. No-one runs it even though quite a few people, both corporate and governmental, would like to. The only restriction at present is that Internet users and providers are subject to the laws that operate in their home country. However, many commentators believe that plans for Internet censorship, control and surveillance are afoot all over the place, and are concerned about this too.

The distinction between global/corporate scale websites and more local/individual sites is also breaking down. Distance really is now no object. If you're surfing in your room in Boysey Idaho, you don't really care whether the pages you're looking at originated in New York, London or KuchiKuchi beach Samoa. Indeed, there's already quite a tradition for obscure little websites achieving cult status and massive traffic from all over the world, by virtue of instantaneous electronic word-of-mouth. One example has been the much celebrated 'I kiss you' site innocently put up by Mahir, a quaintly eccentric chap in Turkey to attract a local girlfriend.

The fact is that this thing works completely differently from anything else we've had before. In terms of human evolution, it's a very interesting phenomenon and this is a very interesting time to be alive. Who knows what effect the Internet will eventually come to have on the overall spiritual development of our species.

For instance, the Web can and does allow the development of many resources that are of particular value to the mind-body-spirit movement, as you will see from the directory at the back of the book. Many of these web resources play a very active and influential role in their respective fields, such as in the arena of green campaigning (see section 26, page 257). As a more poignant example, use of the Web was instrumental in the mass suicide of the Heaven's Gate community in 1999. And there are now sites for survivors of everything from childhood abuse to Siddha Yoga to infant confectionery withdrawal.

The future of the Internet

The nature of the Internet and the World Wide Web are changing, and changing more rapidly, all the time. Perhaps this will continue forever, or perhaps things will settle down and stabilize after a while – rather as they did a while after Mr Gutenberg started printing books in the Middle Ages. We can be sure, though, that things are going to be in a continuing state of flux for quite some time to

come. The key players in the game are still very much jock-
eying for key positions from which to dominate the whole
thing, and big new players are coming in all the time.

No-one is at all sure how the Net is going to develop
from here, but some people are certainly making
informed guesses. These concern such important future
aspects as:

- content of the network;
- ways that this content may be presented;
- methods of accessing it;
- plus a whole variety of human, social and spiritual
  implications about how the whole thing is going to
  affect our lives.

And there is also the question of how we can all exert
influence so that this development is positive and in the
interests of humanity rather than just big business or the
state.

Let's look briefly in turn at these important areas of
prediction.

Future content

One thing's for sure – there's going to be unimaginably
more stuff on the Web than we can conceive of at

present. And it will undoubtedly appear soon in new media formats that are yet to be invented, or are currently in development. For there is at present a hugely under-used potential on the Web, and it's going to get used sooner or later – 'just because it's there', as they said about climbing Mount Everest.

Files are going to go on getting bigger. In the early days of computers, people used to measure electronic information in terms of Bytes and then Kilobytes. This worked for a few years, and then they had to invent Megabytes and use them in ever bigger numbers. After a rather shorter interval, we needed Gigabytes and now Terrabytes. What's going to be next? Perhaps The Simpsons will inspire the next unit of measurement: Overbytes?

So more people will be putting more stuff up there. Probably just about everyone who has a telephone will have a connection to the Web in a relatively short time, and soon after that they'll all have a website too, as well as using email and other web facilities. And they'll be using their website for a wider range of purposes, some of them not yet invented. These will probably relate to every aspect of life – social, family, relationship or romance, career or business, hobbies and interests, sport, holidays, entertainment, fashion, finance, as well as aspects of health, wellbeing and spirituality.

Today, half the people on the Internet are Americans. Eighty-five percent of revenue from Internet businesses goes to American companies. But people in the business are realizing that this market has little growth potential left as about 80 percent of people there are already online. By 2004 it is estimated that only one third will be in US, and two thirds of all spending will be done elsewhere. A few advanced web corporations such as Yahoo! and MSN have already been globalising their businesses for three or four years, so that they are now much visited by users in many different countries. They know that in the not too distant future very few people will care about American content; what they will be interested in is local content. It's beginning to happen already. But there's also likely to be a continuing wave of global mergers.

With all this ever-proliferating content, ranging in quality from the great and priceless to the awful, the useless and worse, it's becoming more and more difficult to separate the wheat from the chaff. If anything, the 'noise to signal ratio' is increasing, and will probably continue to do so. Finding what you want is also becoming ever more difficult in the midst of all this. Current estimates are that only 15 percent of all sites are presently indexed at all, and when they are it is only their 'front pages' that are referred to. There's already talk of creating superior networks that perform better than the Internet we have today. A British entrepreneur has launched something called the Madge Broadcast Network (MBN), bypassing the slow public Net to deliver streaming RealVideo through an **overnet**.

Websites, too, are becoming ever more complex, and an increasing proportion of them are badly designed, as easy-to-use web design tools fall into the hands of all and sundry. Check out, for instance, the worst-designed-sites sources in the directory section of this book for just a few classic examples of this unfortunate genre.

Sites will undoubtedly continue to become increasingly interactive with the user, who will become more and more able to influence its content and format and how to use it, rather than simply visit it as a passive onlooker.

'Content' is becoming the buzzword for people with a web presence. They want you to stay on their site for as long as possible and so they need to keep you enthralled, informed, entertained, amused, distracted or otherwise un-bored for as long as they possibly can. This calls for a lot of 'content' all round. Alongside this, the recent trend has also been towards **portalisation**; all kinds of web pages, browsing tools and other forms of web presence that provide access to additional content and services in addition to their primary purpose. All of these people are trying to create the ultimate web **one-stop-shop**, in competition to everyone else's. And they all want to make inroads into your life, especially at this formative time in the development of the whole Internet, when our habits all are being shaped for the future. Everyone's trying to get in there and stake their claim while it's still fluid, before patterns get hardened and fixed and rankings between competitors are established.

They all want to be your home page. They want to invade your life. They want to be the centre of your world. If you bear this in mind you will better understand why they do things the way they do. And you'll be better able to make choices that suit your needs and your priorities rather than theirs; this is an important part of conscious surfing. The choices you make: hardware, software, browsers, search tools, sites visited and so on – all make a big difference to your own experience, as well as playing a part in influencing how the whole thing develops.

The fact is, you see, that all of this stuff is tending to become more and more intrusive, invasive and manipulative in terms of your computer and your ways of using it. The personal computer is subtly being subsumed by stuff on the Web. Software that you install to access the Web produces significant changes on your own hard drive. The distinction between the contents of your disk and the vast resources of the Web is inexorably becoming blurred. This is certainly going to continue, as the Web browser becomes the kind of tool that you use to find your way around your own files; it will become the main interface between you and your computer. This transition will become more and more invisible, as users find it equally easy to access what is on their computer and what isn't. Then you won't know which you're actually using; material that is downloading from the Web may just be a little slower to bring up on screen. And the next stage will be that it won't even be slower. Your own hard drive will have become a subset of the Web. All this will become more prevalent as telecoms companies restructure their pricing, and new technologies speed up access and deliver better service.

And at present, access between your computer and the Web is more or less one way – you go there – but this too is changing; access the other way without your say-so is on the way. Is all this a bit sinister? It could be; we don't really know yet. It's just unfettered business at work, really. But BBC TV in England recently screened a piece of fiction set in the year 2013, when the Net was portrayed as having developed genuine digital intelligence, and had started to behave independently, beginning with the malignant release of confidential government files and pornography around the world.

Means of access

The rapidly developing means of access themselves will have big influence on future developments. A decade ago, early Net users thought they were lucky to be able to communicate at speeds of 2.4 kilobytes per second, which was just enough to send and receive short text messages. Today, the average home phone line allows transfer at up to 56K/sec. But this is not nearly fast enough to process high quality **streaming audio**, much less the full video that regular modern computers can easily present. This method of access has been replaced in some areas by **ISDN** over the same regular telephone lines, which is a lot faster. This is already being superseded in the US, however, by the use of **ADSL** (asymmetric digital subscriber line), a high-speed cable that gives the much anticipated broadband access. This can currently offer a connection speed of 512K or more, bringing far greater potential transfer in a short download time. It also gives a permanent connection to the Net so you don't need to log on and off or pay metered charges. As it's fast, you can use much the same multimedia applications via the Net as you can on your computer at home. At the end of 2000 it was estimated that there were 1.5 million homes in the US using ASDL. ASDL will make a whole set of new media possibilities viable, such as online TV quality video, video phoning and conferencing and interactive television. Companies and individuals will be able to make full video and multimedia presentations available online instead of their relatively static current offerings, and without slow downloading. So the Net may well become the preferred advertising medium over print or even conventional TV and radio.

The kind of gizmo we use to effect connection to the Net is changing, too. WAP phones are already widely available, and can handle email or download simple information from the Net. But they're looking like a technology that's about to be superseded before they really get established. Mobile phones are already more common than PCs in many regions; in China the ratio is 10 to 1. Some Asian Pacific countries will probably leapfrog the west by adopting mobile phones and palmtop computers for Internet access ahead of computers. Microsoft is making a second big attempt to get into the hand-held market with its new PocketPC operating system for mobile devices, to compete with the dominant Palm Pilot and Psion systems. Gaming computers can access the Net, though the connections are currently relatively show. This is likely to change soon, as Internet gaming develops and a the distinction between using a machine just for Internet and for other functions becomes greater. The PC as a means of getting online will certainly be steadily replaced by something simpler and cheaper, which gets its computer power and intelligence from the network instead of storing it on a local hard drive.

The current network structure based on PCs and local servers will gradually be superseded by Net terminals accessing data and application software that is hosted by secure Internet sites. Such software will be rented, either per user or according to amount of use. **Broadband** access will make all of this suddenly more possible. All of the above will tend to produce a much more network-based commercial society. Indeed, some trend-watchers believe that in only a few years machines rather than people will be the heaviest web users.

More things to worry about

So, is all this going to be good for us? As in most commercial situations, everything is rushing forward blindly. As soon as there is a technical capability of doing something it gets done, whether it's good for humanity or not, because somebody can get in there first, become the biggest and make money out of it – and because of lack of regulation. In the midst of all this hectic feeding frenzy, there are a couple of voices crying out in the cyber wilderness, expressing concern about whether the Net's benefits to humanity will outweigh its disadvantages and dangers. For instance, its development could further polarize society, increasing the gap between the richest and the poorest and between those who have access to the technology and those who haven't. Proponents of alternative approaches to economics (see

http://www.neweconomies.org) argue that people at the margins of society, who could theoretically stand to benefit most, might actually miss out. This concern has led to a number of innovative schemes to get ghetto communities online (see **http://www.redbricks. org.uk**). Ultimately it's up to individuals and alternative organizations such as these to come up with ideas for managing and influencing the development of the Web and to put them into practice, if it isn't to become a total playground for multinational consortia.

The Internet is currently in a phase of extraordinary freedom and possibility, but forces are already at work to exert control over the whole thing. The most influential role in this game resides in creating the software that will come to dominate the Net. The coding of which this software consists embodies these kinds of values. The Internet's original design principle was based on something called end-to-end coding, which ensured that users could choose which applications they wanted to use, rather than network owners making such decisions. This prevented control either by governments or business interests; the whole system was inherently free from local regulation. Broadband cable networks are now building enormous potential influence, with giant mergers of cable and content providers such as that between AT&T and Media One, which grabbed 80 percent of the residential Broadband market. As cable systems and other structures are held in the hands of corporate entities, power can be exerted over what software and technology is used. AOL, for instance, now has half the dial-up users in the world. Potential innovators now need to check whether such systems will support their new ideas and so make them economically viable (see **http://www.cria.org.uk**).

Government control is also beginning to rear its potentially ugly head. The US Supreme Court has ruled that Internet Service Providers are not responsible for libellous remarks made by their clients in email or websites. But in Britain a law is currently going through Parliament, requiring all Internet Service Providers to install tracking software that will enable them to read everything that passes over the Internet, and allow government to tap ISPs, emails, electronic pagers and WAP phones. Similar measures are afoot in certain other countries – and that's only what we know about. The Republic of Ireland, on the other hand, is working to outlaw government snooping on the Net. It's all a bit of a mess, really. If you want to add your voice to the campaign against web censorship, contact the free speech campaign Blue Ribbon Online, at **http://www.eff.org/blueribbon**.

2 surfing the net

In this section, you'll find out:

- how information is stored and connected together on the Web;
- how to find it;
- how to choose and use the software you'll need for this;
- how to keep the good stuff;
- gathering music, video and animation from the Web;
- how to search more effectively;
- what uses you can put your findings to;
- how to avoid undesirable material; and
- get the answers to many frequently asked questions about web searching.

The **World Wide Web** (or **www**) is just one part of the Internet. But in itself it's a vast conglomeration of resources that can be accessed from any point within the network, either to put stuff up there or to get it out.

Much of this content is in the form of visual information, organized into **pages** comprising text and graphics – currently something approaching 1,000 million of them. But there are many other types of data that can be retrieved, such as sound files, moving pictures and combinations of these – all of which now form an increasing proportion of the total. So as well as reading material on the Web, you can hear live radio and music concerts, or sample CDs and movies. All this is evolving and developing all the time, spontaneously creating a relentlessly increasing amount of content and range of formats.

A month is a long time in cyberspace

Yes, it's all changing very, very quickly. New stuff is being put up there every hour of every day, while much that's there already is superseded or withdrawn, or is simply fading away due to lack of upkeep. This means that keeping up to date is a crucial issue in searching the Web. Websites vary wildly in terms of how long they last before mysteriously vanishing. It's interesting to note that many of the most elaborate sites, which can appear in a glorious explosion with all guns blazing, often turn out to be the most short-lived; while many smaller and simpler semi-professional or home-based sites will often prove more durable and reliable. This is partly because the astronomical budgets required to constantly service and update the more lavish sites may not continue to be available. But it's also due to another factor that you will quickly discover when you get surfing; pages that are too complex or heavily laden with sophisticated graphics are simply too slow to **download.** So such sites often receive fewer visitors, and even fewer repeat visitors as a result. And visits to sites are important; the three things that online providers are most concerned with are traffic, traffic and traffic. This is because traffic is what is turned into revenue. And that traffic is you.

So the trick in conducting a search, or otherwise navigating your way round the Web, is in being able to go where you want to go rather than where someone else wants you to go. It's just like 'real life', only more so – the commercial pressures are greater, simply because the Net has arrived almost overnight, and is developing at such a rate that people are inventing more and more cunning and devious means of persuasion about every half hour.

So it's important to know how to find what you want, how to know which is the latest material, how to track it down and how to get it onto your screen. The following section shows you how to do this.

The gentle art of browsing

Whatever form the material on the Web takes, it's all connected together and accessed in fundamentally the same way. The main piece of computer software used to access it is the browser. Moving round and sampling content is known as browsing, as if one was a sort of leisurely grazing animal. The key element in moving easily from one site to another is called a link; when you're browsing, you can click on this to immediately jump to another site that may be elsewhere on the same site, or could equally well originate on the other side of the planet. So first of all, let's look at how to browse, and then consider how to find the best pastures to feed on.

Okay, so how do I browse? The browser is the single most essential piece of Internet software. With or without extra bits and pieces fitted, it enables you to find your way around the Web. Here's how it works. A number of different commercial browsers are available, but let's look at their common principles before examining their respective merits.

At its simplest, the browser is something you tell where you want to go. When you launch the program, a default home page appears. This is your starting point for all searches, and the point to which you return. If you know a web address or URL (Uniform Resource Locator), you can key this into the space at the top of the page. URLs can take different forms, according to the type of organization that created the site and what country it is based in. But they are nearly always structured something like this: **http://www.zenteabags.com**. Or else they may be longer, such as: **http://www.homepages.pavilion.co.uk/gerry/**.

When you've typed in this information to the address panel, press Enter or Carriage Return, and the browser should connect to that site and download its pages. You will see the coding for these individual pages appearing at the bottom of your browser window, together with a running report on how much of the info has been downloaded. If the connection isn't successfully made, refer to the possible solutions on page 51. If you don't have an address to key in, check the information below on search tools.

With the more up-to-date versions of the major browser software, you'll find that you don't need to key in the whole of the website address. You can skip out the **http://www.** at the start, and sometimes even the **.com** or other ending. Simply key in the central portion, leaving the browser to add the remainder automatically. However, you will need to enter any capitals correctly, or the connection may not work. The simplest way around all this is to use the computer to copy addresses from wherever you found them, and then paste them into the browser address line. Alternatively, you can click on them when you find them as a link from another site. More on using links later.

Nowadays you can even get a browser that will read the content of web pages aloud to you. Premo Web Talkster (**http://www.webtalkster.com**) is an example of this. It isn't the perfect program yet, but it's a step in the right direction.

The fine art of using links. Links are the key element in navigating round the Web. A link is anything that will lead you to another location; it may take the form of a key word, a URL or website address, an image, a button, or something else that's been invented since this book was written. Whatever form it takes, though, you'll know that it will work as a link because if it's text it will always be underlined and because when you drag your cursor across it with your mouse, the arrow will change into a little hand. If you click when you see the hand, the link will take you to the connected location. Links can be established by one organization within its own material, or by agreement between different organizations. Commercial people are beginning to find cunning ways to exploit links to lead surfers away from competitors' sites to their own, leading to a number of recent court cases. Law enforcers are having to make things up as they go along on matters such as these.

You can usually check in advance where a link is going to take you before doing so; just place the cursor over the link without clicking, and look down to the bottom of the browser window where you will see the linked address appear. These days, however, those same cunning and devious entrepreneurs are finding ways to prevent you getting this little piece of information so that you actually have to follow the link to find out where it goes; that way they have you in their clutches that little bit longer.

What is bookmarking? When you visit a site that you think you may want to go back to later, you can automatically record its address in your browser's memory for future use. According to which program you're using, this is called **Bookmark** or **Favorite** in the browser's pulldown menus. Building up and organizing your library of important bookmarks is a key component of effective surfing.

Which browsing software should I use? This is one of the Big Questions in the surfer's life. In practice, the choices open to you will have already been influenced by the age and capacity of your existing computer hardware and its **operating system,** for instance Macintosh or Windows.

The two giants in the field are **Netscape** which is operated by AOL, and **Internet Explorer**, owned by Microsoft. Both are constantly being updated, with significantly new features for each version. These two browser names are used so much in Internet parlance that they're commonly abbreviated to, for instance, **NS6** or **IE5.1**. There are also a number of 'independent' browsers such as **Opera**. If you have an older computer set-up, you'll have to use earlier versions rather than these latest memory-guzzling monsters, loaded as they are with bells, whistles and miscellaneous **plug-ins,** which you may or may not want.

A brief history of the browser wars

An early version of Netscape Navigator was the first commercially oriented browser. Before the advent of the commercial browser, the Internet was accessed on an ad hoc one-to-one basis by computer freaks and online organizations, with bulletin boards for communal links. Then Netscape developed HTML commercially, and was able to dominate the market.

Netscape Navigator went through a number of versions until in 1997 version 3 was mysteriously replaced by something called Netscape Communicator, with a new portal style website format. Eventually Microsoft decided that it should have a browser too, and this quickly became a serious competitor and evolved through many different versions.

With the might of the Microsoft corporation against it, Netscape has taken some serious bashing over the years, but in 1999 it was taken over by the giant Internet presence of AOL. NC got up to version 4 and for a while didn't really come out with any significant updates to match Explorer. Recently, however, Netscape has unaccountably leapt forward to version 6, leaving out version 5. Somewhat confusingly too, the new version is neither Navigator nor Communicator – it's just Netscape 6.

The question of how to choose between NS and IE, then, depends to a significant degree on which versions of each is being considered, which in turn could be influenced by hardware restrictions mentioned above. However, some broad observations may be made in comparing the latest versions. Some of these are listed here; others are mentioned under specific headings elsewhere in the book.

Some broad observations:

- IE has been thought by many to lead in terms of features and ease of use. It is seamlessly built in to the Windows operating system, interlocking with other Microsoft software such as Word for Windows, Excel etc.
- It has a rather large package of supplementary tools, not all of which, though, may be necessary.
- It has a sophisticated facility for automating Internet tasks, known as Intellisense.
- There is a comprehensive in-depth help menu.

- Its cumbersome overall size can take up excessive disk
  space and produce slower downloading of web pages.

IE also incorporates **Outlook Express**, its dedicated email
program. Many users favour this, although it has turned
out to be consistently hackable and prone to security and
virus problems. Some users feel, too, that IE is developing
overall in a way that is excessively invasive and limiting of
choice within the hosting computer resources; IE also has
a built-in feature that can check out details of what software you have on your hard drive, and send this information back to Microsoft HQ. However, you can disable this
if you wish. Others simply prefer not to support Microsoft
– especially Mac freaks.

At the time of going to press, Microsoft has launched
IE5.5 for Windows, an interim upgrade which includes
improved support for printing, and purportedly offers
richer browsing experience through enhanced DHTML
features and additional visual effects processing. The
simultaneous upgrade for Mac users, IE5, is a significant
improvement on the less stable (i.e. liable to crash) and
more bug-prone version 4.5

In the world of Netscape browsing, the new version 6 is
where attention is now being focused. By the time you
read this, the 'program formerly known as Netscape

Communicator' is likely to be out in its final form as NS6, promising to improve significantly on previous releases in terms of speed, stability, special features and compatibility with web systems. A number of major steps forward are claimed:

- **My Sidebar** is a separate collapsible panel that appears to the side of the main browser window. It can hold different types of content, which remain when the main view changes as other pages are loaded. This can contain bookmarks, search tools, or customized information from other websites, such as news headlines or quotations from the stock market. Content providers such as CNN are being encouraged to offer material that automatically keys into this sidebar. If NS6 succeeds in building a dedicated following, other content providers will no doubt find it worthwhile to come up with such material for this application.
- For those with concerns about privacy and security, NS6 provides a **cookie manager** (see page 53 for further information on cookies). This allows you to view and selectively delete any cookies that the browser identifies, and choose to accept or reject them on a site-by-site basis. A **password manager** stores the user name and password that you use as needed for each particular site, eliminating the need to remember them individually. IE5 does this too.

- The email application lets you manage a number of email accounts from within your **user profile**, supporting different types of mail including POP, IMAP and AOL, and promising **web mail accounts** (see email, page 66) in the future. Each of your **email identities** has its own separate facility for sending and receiving mail. IE's Outlook Express has had a similar feature for some time, but NS enables the very great number of AOL email users worldwide to use the **Instant Messenger** service as well. This means that you can have instantaneous and unbroken to-and-fro messaging conversations with other AOL/NS6 users if they happen to be online at the time, without dialling up again for replies. There is also a feature for collected addresses which automatically keeps a copy of the address of anyone who sends you an email – a useful back-up facility in case you delete a message without saving their details into your address book.
- The problems of downloading a browser from the Net in the first place have been addressed by NS6 features. Installation starts with a very small document of only 200 or 300 Kbytes, which allows you to choose which components of the main browser you wish to receive, only forcing on you the relatively compact core components. Furthermore the **Smart Update** feature allows pausing and later resuming of downloading if the online connection is lost – a relatively common occurrence.

- Probably the most significant new feature of NS6 is its greatly enhanced degree of **standards compliance**, meaning that more stuff that you encounter on the Net is going to be compatible and therefore successfully downloadable. This is because NS6 is built around Gecko layout technology, from the universally accepted **open source** (i.e. not owned by any company) Mozilla project.
- The Mozilla connection provides another feature, the highly customizable **user interface**. This enables users to choose from a variety of different interface styles or **skins**, which incorporate a range of desktop themes, icons etc. You can now even disguise your Netscape browser as an Explorer browser, if that sort of thing turns you on. There is also multi-platform compatibility – NS6 is available for Windows, Macintosh and even Linux operating systems. Unfortunately NS6 has attracted some bad press because of proneness to bugs.

Is that a browser in your pocket or are you just pleased to see me? Both of these major browsers are relatively bloated monsters that gobble up large amounts of space on your hard drive and use a lot of memory in their operation. But there are alternatives. Perhaps the most notable of these is Opera, which is small and compact; many people find that it can do what they want. Opera lacks support for Java, so you won't see these on any sites that use it. Lynx is a text-only browser. If you have limited hard disk space or memory, or don't need a lot of auto-mated functions and you don't want to support a global mega-corporation, this could be a viable option. The lower need for memory and hard disk space can be especially valuable on a notebook computer, especially if it's not the latest model. And getting rid of the fancy features does mean that you can download and display web pages a lot faster. About 15 percent of people use the independent browsers rather than the big two. You can find evaluations of browsers at **http://www.browserwatch.internet.com**.

Up-to-date versions of the major browsers, including the independent ones, are easily obtainable on free CDs with Internet magazines. But if you want to download them for free, or have a choice of different versions, you can go to the sites listed on page 44.

Adapting your browser

You can do a great deal, if you so wish, to alter a variety of settings which your browser incorporates, so that it performs in ways that suit you better. This involves varia-tions on the **default settings** chosen by the software company, which are not always ideal.

For instance, you can change the **default home page** – what you see when you open the browser – and change it to whatever you want instead. That might be, for instance, the home page of a site you visit often, or of your preferred search engine (see page 44). Or you could choose for the browser to always open on whichever page you were last at on your previous surfing session. Probably best of all, choose the 'blank page' option, which will be the fastest loading of the lot.

Adjustments to settings are made in slightly different ways in different browsers:

- In IE pull down the Tools menu and click on 'Internet Options'.
- In NS pull down the Edit menu and select 'Preferences'.

Browsing can be speeded up dramatically by choosing the 'advanced browser' settings such as:

- 'not showing images' i.e. text only; or
- 'not showing multimedia' (see below).

Other settings that you can change affect privacy and security. Guidelines on choosing these are dealt with on pages 58 to 63.

So go on – exercise your rights to have things the way you want them, rather than the way some omnipotent corporation wants you to have them – for reasons we won't begin to understand until it's too late.

Remembering where the good stuff is

The easy way to make sure that you can always find a site again is to get into the habit of bookmarking while you're at it in the first place. Bookmarking is a crucial surfing activity, and you should do it all the time. When you find yourself at any page that you may want to be able to revisit, just click on:

- 'Favorites' in IE
- 'Bookmarks' in NS

The page's URL will be saved onto your hard disk. When you've gathered a lot of these, which you will if you surf at all, it's important to employ some method of organizing them. The simplest approach is to use the browser's built-in facility for sorting them into folders, using either the browser's lists or your own purpose-made categories.

Another possibility is to use a desktop-based accessory such as Powermarks (**http://www.kaylon.com/power.html**) to grab links from your browser and arrange them into a manageable format. There are even web-based services for organizing bookmarks such as Backflip (**http://www.backflip.com**) and Blink (**http://www.blink.com**), which import your existing favourites and automatically organize them by category into a kind of personalized portal. Finally, there are web thingies that can learn from your surfing habits and help you. Deepleap (**http://www.deepleap.com**) organizes details of the sites you visit most often. And Spyonit (**http://www.spyonit.com**) lets you know when your favourite websites have been updated so you can go and see them again.

But there are other ways of finding previously visited sites, especially those that you've been to recently. The key to this is to make use of your browser's 'History' facility – its own record of where you've just been, and in which precise sequence. There are several ways of using the history file:

- To go back to a page you visited in the same surfing session, click on the 'Back' button at the top of the browser window. For a page visited later in the sequence press 'Forward', and navigate to and fro in this way. The 'Home' button takes you to a home page that you can specify in your browser, and 'Stop' interrupts the current page loading.
- If you can't find the required page, you can click on History in the drop-down menu and make a direct search. This can show you links that you've recently visited in different colours according to how long ago

it was. History files can grow to a size that slows down your web searches, so you may have to reduce them from time to time, or adjust your preferences so that history links are kept for a shorter time.

Offline browsing at your leisure

Your browser, then, automatically keeps a record of all the sites and pages you've visited recently. When you go back to one of these, you'll notice that the page loads much more quickly than the first time. That's because the browser has temporarily kept all its data in its **cache**, a short-term memory bank. And this data can be preserved even when you go **offline**. So you can speedily gather up any interesting looking pages while you're browsing without looking too closely, and then read them later when you've gone offline. To do this, choose 'Work Offline' from the File menu. Once you're offline, you can read the pages already downloaded by:

- keying in the desired address;
- clicking on them in the history window;
- navigating around with the Back or Forward buttons; or
- following links within pages that you're already viewing.

IE 5 has a particularly good reputation for searching the contents of pages that have been stored in the cache.

A number of settings for the cache can be adjusted by changing your preferences.

Some people even set their computers so that the browser can capture slow-loading pages during the night, for offline viewing the following day. Downloading can be a lot faster worldwide while America sleeps. You can also choose to download some pages in the background while browsing, or while reading on screen other pages that you've already downloaded, on the screen. Opening multiple sites is achieved by choosing the 'New Window' option. Madly keen mega-surfers are developing these habits, but they are quickly being adopted by less dysfunctional types, because there is simply so much stuff out there to check out, and it would be really awful to miss something, wouldn't it?

Browser add-ons and plug-ins

Modern versions of the big-boy browsers now come equipped with a host of plug-in software **attachments** that go way beyond viewing regular text and pictures. If you have a browser version that doesn't include them, you can download them individually from the Web. Popular plug-ins include:

- **RealAudio** which activates sound content from websites;

- **WinAmp** (Windows format) and **MacAmp** (Mac format), which gives access to **MP3** music files, all the rage now for music downloading, at **http://www.winamp.com** and **http://www.macamp.com**;
- **RealVideo**, activating video clips;
- **Shockwave** Macromedia and **Flash** plug-ins, for viewing multimedia presentations.

These gizmos enable you, for instance, to view animations, listen to concerts or live radio, or view movie clips – all for free. When you encounter a site which calls for one of these and you don't already have it, you may be automatically offered the opportunity to do so. But see page 58 for security aspects of downloading software.

Search tools

Search engines and their various relatives form the most important starting point for web searching, but variations on them are developing very fast.

A search engine is a website that finds the sites you want from data you give it about your search criteria and subject preferences. Sidebar, on page 35, lists some of the most important of these, together with details of how they can be obtained online. Once you've entered your search **keywords** into the search engine, it hunts around the Web to find the pages that most closely match your requirements. At least, that's what it appears to be doing – in fact, it's actually checking its own offline archives which have been selected from the Web at some point in the past. So in practice, these will always be incomplete and out of date to some degree; this is one of the key criteria for choosing a search engine. You are then presented with a set of search results – a series of site URLs that are ranked in order of how closely the engine thinks they match your request. To visit any of these links, you simply click on it. Search tools vary widely in terms of how they choose and present these results. And some are more oriented towards finding commercial sites, while others can be better for finding factual or educational information. The best advice is to try them out and use those that best suit your own preferences, and the kind of information you're looking for at any particular time. You pay your money and you take your pick (except that most of them are actually free). There is an in-depth guide to search engines at **http://www.webreference.com/content/search**. There are country-specific versions of some engines, such as **http://www.excite.co.uk** and **http://www.yahoo.co.uk**. For further afield, **http://www.twics.com/~takakuwa/search** has links to engines from Afghanistan to Zimbabwe.

When looking for sites with a common theme, a category based resource such as Yahoo! or About.com can be useful. Searches can also be geographically significant. For instance, UKMax is useful when you specifically want to eliminate information that concerns USA – by far the greater part of material on the Web. You can find up-to-date information on the latest engines, together with hints and tips on using them, at **http://www.searchengineswatch.com**. For searches in the mind-body-spirit field, there will also be some very specific search tools that will be particularly helpful. These are listed in the directory section in Part 2. For finding specialist sites, check out specialist engines at **http://www.searchenginewatch.com** or **http://www.searchenginesgalore.com** – especially if you want to find people, addresses or phone numbers.

Speed and volume of results might seem to be an obvious advantage, but bear in mind that the engines that promise the greatest numbers of **hits** or the shortest response times also tend to be the least discriminating and least accurate in coming up with what you really want.

A few years ago, some bright spark invented the portal and all of a sudden the bigger search engines too began to offer news, email and entry to numerous other services. This can create desktop clutter that really only gets in the way of serious searching. Another problem is that porn-merchants have become adept at adding bogus keyword **tags** to their pages, so that a perfectly innocent search can bring some heavy duty grunge onto your screen. Just remember not to save it onto your hard drive.

Directories

Directories are another resource that you can use for online searching. Using them, you get results that are shorter but better, because of the human element used in compiling them. They're good for looking for major pages on a major topic. If you want to search all over the Web for a particular phrase or topic, it will be better to use a search engine. But directories are often the best means of locating a specialized site or range of sites within a given specific topic. They can also be good for getting to the newest information. They're usually sorted by subject, date or other relevant criteria. For even more specialized or newer subjects, mini-directories may be found. You might want to contribute to one of these yourself, if you're an expert or if your own website is relevant. Lists of directories can be found at sites such as **http://www.super-seek.com** or **http://www.webdata.com**. An extensive range of directories that are relevant to mind-body-spirit subjects are given in the directory section on page 110. When looking for any kind of directory, the Open Directory Project is always worth checking out at **http://www.dmoz.org**. Yahoo! and Lycos aren't really search engines – they're directories.

But the best way round the limitations of individual tools such as search engines, databases and directories is to use a resource that draws on multiple sources and then collates the results for you. These are variously referred to as **meta search engines** or **search agents**. You can sometimes end up with extremely long lists of results. Here too, the question of which one will work best for you depends on your purpose and your preferences:

- **Google** is a very popular choice for general purposes and for information gathering. Google has led the way in the anti-portal backlash, and offers web searching that is stripped back to its simple essentials. It works out which are going to be the most useful for your keyword input, based on the number of people who are already linking to the sites it comes up with – a good way of reducing the ubiquitous crap factor that regular search engines are subject to. Google has a new index which contains a billion Internet addresses. They say this is equivalent to searching a stack of paper more than 70 miles high in half a second.
- **AltaVista** followed this trend, launching RagingSearch (**http://www.raging.com**) as a pared-down alternative to its main portal style search site.
- **Dogpile** can be good for finding more commercial sites, and for fun stuff.
- **Ask Jeeves** doesn't give access to a great number of search engines, and is not terribly easy to get the hang of immediately, but can be handy for very specific advice or questions like 'Where can I find local pain-free yoga classes?'

- One of the best of all these search agents is **Copernic 2000**, which is thorough and extremely versatile, submitting queries to a dozen or more of the best regular search engines. You can get it to work in whichever way suits your own individual purposes; for instance, ask it to search the Web generally, or look for music pages only, or for people. It presents the results in a very efficient and usable way. As with Google, some searchers use nothing else. Copernic can be downloaded for free, but the purchasable version has some extra and very worthwhile features.

To find other search agents, visit either:

- http://www.comparenet.com
- http://www.stroud.com or
- http://www.tucows.com

Other search facilities that are now appearing carry search possibilities still further, and continue the ever-increasing blurring of the distinction between files on your own hard drive and on everyone else's. Autonomy's **Kenjin** is a forerunner in this area. It runs in the background as you go about your regular business, pulling out suggestions from the Web or from your own hard drive when they seem to be relevant to your current project. Its toolbar sits on your desktop, stealthily watching the information you view and the words you type – learning all about you and then making suggestions as to where you can find information which it thinks will interest you. You don't even have to ask it. Spooky, or what? Kenjin claims to offer greater accuracy of searching than other resources, by working with words in their specific context, and taking account of whole sentences or even entire documents before making a search. It is relatively compact – 1.5Mb – and it's free. It's intelligent and fully configurable. This sort of thing may point the way to the future of searching, but at present it doesn't mark the end of conventional search engines. It could well be a very useful complement to them, however. Perhaps one could think of it as a kind of interested electronic mother-in-law.

Other means of searching can apply when you want to search Usenet, newsgroup or email resources. These can often uncover fresher information on new subjects or resources. They are covered in Chapters 3 and 4.

All these search sites, like many other web presences, are aspirational. They are constantly trying to turn them-selves into all you will ever need on the Internet. They see themselves as homes for lost souls. They want to be the starting point for all your Net activities. In other words, they want to be Your Home Page. This is the phenomenon of rampant portalisation. Other sites do this by somewhat pretentiously calling themselves **hubs** or **communities** – terms that often don't mean very much other than having extra features with which they hope to attract visitors.

There are also lots of specialized list/sites that you can consult, such as 'Cool Site of the Day'.

Note: If you're searching for the answer to a question that is likely to be frequently asked, you could try one of the frequently-asked-question sites, such as **http://www.faq.org**.

Hints and tips on effective searching

- Choosing your search keywords carefully is crucial to effective searching. Use the least general and most specific terms that you can possibly think of, in order to catch what you want and weed out what you don't.
- With many search engines, you can add **Boolean Operators** to make the search even more precise and exclusive. These include terms such as AND or NOT. If two words read together can make the search more accurate than if they were separate, put them within inverted commas, as in 'yoga holidays'.
- Spread your search. Use a variety of search engines or search agents to do it for you. Focus on those that

have worked for you in the past, for each particular
type of search activity that you do regularly.

- If you don't find what you are looking for in fifteen
  minutes, go down to the local library instead.

**What do I do if I've got the address but still can't
find the site?** If you key a URL into your browser but
it can't find the page, perhaps getting the dreaded
error message '404 not found', there are several possible explanations and options for what you can do
about it:

- The address could be incorrect; check with the source.
  Remember that it's always simpler and more accurate
  to click on a link, make a bookmark, or copy and paste
  the URL from wherever you found it directly into your
  browser than to key it in afresh. If you have to do this,
  make sure you get any capitalization and punctuation
  marks exactly correct.
- If it still doesn't work, try variations on the name in
  case you or someone else has spelt it wrong. Also try
  variations on the end coding, such as .co.uk instead of
  .com or vice versa, or try different country codes.
- Very many sites simply go out of date or change their
  names, leaving **dead addresses** or **broken links** as
  their pages are removed from the Web. Others still exist
  as a site and home page, but have different page URLs,

so try deleting the portions of the URL following the '/' symbol, and try again.

- Sometimes a browser can malfunction – if it fails on a number of consecutive addresses, close it down, restart the computer and open it again.

- The host you are trying to connect to may be overloaded with traffic. Try at another time (such as when North America is asleep).

How to avoid what you don't want

The previous section has explained how to find the sites you want, and avoid the sites that don't contain what you're looking for. But there are certain other web presences that you may wish not to encounter. These are, in approximate order of potential notoriety:

- cookies;
- advertising;
- unsolicited pornography;
- the much-hated spam;
- security breaches;
- and the dreaded virus.

What are cookies, and who bakes them? Cookies are small pieces of computer coding that are placed on your hard drive by your browser at the instigation of a site as you visit it. This data includes a unique ID which enables the site to recognize you when you return, and may include information about what you were interested in, what purchases you made and so on. Cookies represent another little facet of the ongoing breakdown in barriers between data on your own computer and on the Internet. Purveyors of cookies, and many Net commentators, argue that this is a totally benign process, that it enables you to get a more efficient service, and that it speeds up service because things don't have to start from scratch again when you revisit a site. Furthermore, they say, no cookie can be read by any site other than the one that put it there. However, many surfers don't like it on principle, and consider that the whole thing is an unacceptable intrusion and threat to privacy. Consumer groups and regulators on both sides of the Atlantic are getting edgy. A Californian woman has filed a lawsuit against DoubleClick, the Web advertising giant, accusing them of using cookies to unlawfully obtain and sell private information. Some see them as the thin end of the wedge, wondering how such a seemingly innocent use of such facilities may develop and be used in the future. For instance, some ISPs already track your online movements using this kind of information. There are fears at websites such as Cookie Central (**http://www.cookiecentral.com**) that they might be developed to snoop through PCs looking for a bank balance, for instance. Most leading websites use cookies.

Cookies are really the online equivalent of the information that mailshot operators try to gather about people in order to target customers; so it's information that people will pay money for, like conventional mailing lists but potentially far more valuable. Commercial interest like this in consumer **traffic** is precisely what is driving the development of the whole Internet at such breakneck speed.

If you don't like cookies, the answer is to use the settings in your browser to control them. You can either have all cookies rejected, or set it to give you a warning when a site is trying to send you one, and then choose to accept or reject it according to what you feel about the site in question. Some people find it simpler to allow all cookies and then delete them daily using the menu facility provided.

Avoiding unwanted advertising

Just as in 'real life', commercial organizations want to advertise on the Web. And since in business you rarely get something for nothing, advertising presence is often the price you pay for getting a product or service for 'free'. It's something we're going to be seeing a lot more of, you can be sure.

Banner ads are one of the most common formats; when you click on them, you're led to pages about the advertised item. Nobody ever clicks on them, but they're still all over the place. No doubt somebody is coming up with something far more devious and cunning right now. In the meantime, there are a number of things you can do about unwanted advertising:

- Avoid search engines that sponsor it.
- Choose your search keywords accurately to avoid bringing up commercial sites that are trying to sell you something that isn't relevant to your search.
- Use a purpose-made utility such as **Adsoff**! This nifty little piece of software (1.47Mb) removes banner ads, pop-up windows in web pages, and even cookies and tracking by ISPs. It works away in the background as you surf. Adsoff! currently costs about £12 (US$20) but should be well worth it if this matter is a priority for you. It's available at **http://www.intercantech.com**.

Smut happens

Pornography sites have an uncanny habit of popping up on your screen when you've requested something as innocent as 'vegetarian sausages'. Freud might argue that it's all the result of your deeply suppressed unconscious desires; but the more likely explanation is that unscrupulous pornmongers get you to look at their wares by placing could-be-innocent-could-be-otherwise keywords in the meta-tags that they supply for their sites to the search engines. It's a bit like the 'real world' again, where bona fide massage practitioners have to be careful using words like 'relief' in their publicity.

The threat of accidentally downloading porn is a great concern for many people, particularly if children are going to be using the computer. There are several steps you can take to minimize this intrusion:

- Install filtering software that can prevent access to known porn material; examples include **CyberSnoop** and **CyberPatrol**, or **Kiddesk** with children in mind generally.
- Make your dissatisfaction clear to your ISP.
- See a psychiatrist.

Spam, spam, glorious spam

Spam has greater power to evoke frenzied rage and bitter hatred in an otherwise calm and civilized web surfer than any other of the considerable causes of annoyance that the Net provides. **Spam** is unsolicited advertising email sent out in bulk by parties who have obtained your email address by inappropriate means. People who do it are called **spammers**, as in the commonly used phrase, 'Die spammers, die!' The term derives from the infamous Monty Python song, for early net-geeks were heavily into Python instead of having girlfriends or going out.

If you're troubled by repeated spam-attacks, here's what you can do:

- Not reply. Replying to spam, even to say 'stop it', doesn't work on automatic commercial spammers; it only confirms that your address is valid and draws more. 'Unsubscribing' usually does work.
- If someone spams you repeatedly and won't stop, you can complain to their ISP whose details appear in the spamming email, and have them kicked out.
- In the IE browser, you can set up a filter to weed out particularly offending spammings.
- Certain websites are available to supply you with hints, tips and software downloads, as well as passionate outpourings on the subject.

Security alert. Computer security is a source of increasing concern to aware surfers. Aspects that involve credit card details are dealt with under Internet shopping (page 86). Apart from viruses, the other main risk to security is in downloading software from the Web. Nowadays it is perfectly possible for someone to supply a program which, when you've installed it, can acquire data from your hard drive and send it back to the perpetrators when you're online again. In order to minimize this risk:

- Only download software from reputable sources.

- If you're unsure about whether the source organization is reputable, find out more about it. Exchange email with them, try to discover their physical location, and then make a judgement from your impressions.
- If in the slightest doubt – read my lips – 'just say no'.

Horrid, horrid viruses

A so-called computer virus is a piece of programming that installs itself on your hard drive without your knowledge, disrupting its workings in a number of possible ways. Viruses are usually designed to automatically distribute themselves to other computers – hence the name. They are written deliberately by very clever but probably unhappy people. Perhaps they've suffered in a past lifetime at the hands of a torturer who has now reappeared at the head of a large software corporation, and this is their chance for revenge.

The effects of viruses varies greatly. Some are relatively innocent; they just get into your system and say, 'Hey look – I got into your system!' Some insert bizarre phrases into Microsoft Word files. Some replicate themselves so many times that they bring the whole operating system to a halt; they're often called worms because of this burrowing habit. Some can wipe a whole hard drive clean. The notorious 'I love you' virus of early 2000 caused billions of dollars worth of damage worldwide.

Viruses were first passed around on floppy disks, then on CDRoms, Zip disks and other transferable media, and this is still a very real possibility. But the worldwide epidemics that now take place almost overnight are perpetrated by fantastic creations that transmit themselves automatically across whole sectors of the Internet. So nowadays the most common way of getting a virus is by downloading an infected file from the Web, or by opening an email attachment. If you received the Melissa virus of 1999, it would have sent itself to everyone on your entire email address book as soon as you opened it. So most people would have passed it on even before it had taken effect on their own system. In fact, many viruses are present for long periods of time, being passed on, without the computer user being aware. The more recent **VBS Kakworm** propagated itself through an ActiveX control embedded in OE5.0 emails. When a sufferer boots up their PC, they get an error window that says 'Kagou-Anti-Kro$oft says not today!', whereupon the machine shuts down. To fix it, the user has to start up the machine from a CD-ROM system disk, update both IE and OE, scan for the virus and then follow instructions downloaded from the appropriate site on the Web.

Macintosh computers are infinitely more immune to the depredations of viruses than Windows PC systems. This is partly because their operating systems are better constructed with less potential weakness, but also because the perpetrators may want to do more damage by going for the more popular system – or maybe they're just not very sympathetic with the whole Microsoft approach to business and life. Microsoft Outlook, Word and Excel are the most vulnerable programs. Once a virus has been identified by such a software manufacturer, it can usually produce a **fix** very quickly, and then offer it free for downloading on the Web, for sufferers to run in order to 'disinfect' their system.

With people being online for longer periods, and even permanently online with broadband connections, the risk of someone hacking into a home PC is greatly enhanced. The solution is to build a **firewall**, which businesses have been using for some time to prevent unauthorized access to their systems and networks from the Internet. Firewalls can also prevent users from accessing and tampering with website content. An example program for the home PC user is Norton Internet Security (**http://www.symantec.com**). You have to pay for it. You can find a list of public domain and shareware Internet security software at **http://www.alw.nih.gov/Security/prog-full**. There are quite a few free security guides that you can download from the digital certificate company VeriSign at **http://www.verisign.com**. And you can find out a great deal about Internet security in general at **http://www.iss.net**.

Here's what to do to minimize problems from viruses:

- Install anti-virus software on your computer, and keep it updated regularly from the manufacturer's website. Some programs possess an 'Auto update' facility.
- Use the anti-virus software regularly to scan your hard drive, and set it to check incoming material automatically.
- Keep your browser up to date as well.
- Pay particular attention to data that comes to you on any kind of disk or removable storage medium.
- Don't even think about opening an email attachment unless you know it's okay. It now also seems that viruses can be carried within the body of email messages, if they use HTML coding.   -
- Also pay attention to **executable files** such as web or video files – those whose names end with a dot and three letters, as in .exe.
- Visit **http://Swww.4virus.4anything.com**, which has links to the best anti-virus software, security specialists and other virus information sites.
- Back up all your essential personal documents, and get into the habit of updating the backup regularly, so that you can restore them if they get lost or corrupted. You'll sleep better at night. You don't necessarily need to backup system folders or application software, which you can always reinstall from the original disks.

- If you receive a virus and you know whom you got it from, tell them. If you think you've meanwhile passed it on to anyone else, tell them also. If you now have information on how to fix it, pass that on too. Vow to be a better person, do your virus checking and be more careful in future.
- If you're depressed about it, get counselling.
- If you're a counsellor yourself, consider setting up as a post-viral-depression therapist instead – there's good money in it.

How to keep what you find

Once you've found what you're looking for on the Web – or perhaps something even better – there are several ways that you can process it, as opposed to just reading it and going offline:

- You can print pages directly while you're online, or while offline browsing (see page 42) as long as they're in your History file. All the usual printer parameters such as margins and so on can be adjusted as for normal printing.
- You can save material to your hard drive from pages that you're viewing by selecting and then using the 'Save as' facility. You can save text, images, sound files or other items, as long as you have the corresponding software for these (see pages 43–4).

- In IE you can save a whole website at once, and choose whether you want to keep it as plain text, as HTML for website construction, or **web archive**. You can have all these pages linked as on a live site, and thus browse it offline, even if it is no longer in your History file. And you can drag links into a temporary **clip holder**.
- You can use the browser's automatic facility for passing on links you like to other people who are in your email address book.
- And of course you can spend money and buy things.

Strategies for an ever-changing Internet

The content of the Web is changing rapidly; sites come and go. But there are a number of simple strategies you can incorporate in your surfing and searching habits that will minimize this problem. Much of the material listed in this book has been selected and arranged with these principles in mind.

1 Focus on learning to use search engines and other search tools rather than relying solely on a repertoire of favourite individual sites. Get to know, and bookmark, the search tools that consistently find the kind of results you want.

2 Bookmark and regularly use the sites that tend to be the most long-lived and least transient. This applies

especially to the big specialist MBS portal sites (see page 110) that have already been around for a while, rather than the kind of site that is generated by someone on the spur of the moment and may be dropped next week. The more reliable sites often tend to be on reputable servers and online communities like geocities, tripod, xoom or .about. Learn to spot these address elements in URLs. Organizations and educational establishments also tend to be more stable as a rule.

3 When you find sites that have the quality and attributes that you usually appreciate, which might for instance mean good information rather than poor commercial content with lots of unwanted ads, use their links as much as possible rather than always searching blindly. These sites are usually very selective about the links they accept, and some even use a voting system among their users to evaluate proposed linkages. This applies particularly in the MBS field, where ethics are often an issue. So you get a kind of inbuilt quality control mechanism that can seriously reduce the crap factor.

3 email

Email, or electronic mail, is the single most popular usage of the Internet, even ahead of surfing the Web. There are quite a few reasons why people like to use it:

- It's quicker and easier to use than any other method of sending written mail. It's also simple and easy to learn. Most new people who go online start sending email immediately, but don't get surfing for a while.
- It can be sent, received and replied to almost instantaneously.
- It's very inexpensive, as transmission times for messages are extremely short and are charged at local rates or for free.
- Unlike the telephone, the person you want to communicate with doesn't have to be available at the same time as you. You can send messages to and fro throughout the day, whenever each of you has the opportunity.

- The text of your message is received in electronic form, so that the receiver can use it for other purposes without keying it in. Likewise, all sorts of other usable files can be sent as attachments to the basic message – graphics, sound files, animations, composite materials and so on.
- Many people respond more quickly to emails, often checking it ahead of regular mail, phone messages or fax, which used to be the best way to catch someone's attention.

So email is becoming the next big communication medium. You can now send and receive email from cyber-cafes and from mobile devices like phones and palmtop computers as well as from your desktop at home or work. The format of email messaging is likely to quickly become more sophisticated. Expect to receive an increasing amount of email that arrives in HTML format, just like a web page, with inbuilt photos or graphics, hypertext links to audio or video and other types of content. Email is now also beginning to be able to read out its content to you in simulated voice. Isn't that sweet?

How to use email

Email is handled by your computer either through a **standalone** program or by an emailer that is meshed into the browser, as is Outlook Express with IE.

- **Eudora** is an efficient and reputable choice for those who want an independent emailer that can be used alongside any browser. There is a Light version that can be obtained for free, and a Pro version with more advanced features.
- OE is a popular choice for those who want seamless operation within the IE browser and the whole Windows world. It's particularly good for handling multiple email accounts, but notoriously vulnerable to hacking and viruses (see page 59).
- NS has its own email software in Messenger, which is often the most reliable option for normal everyday use.

Web-based email is an alternative to regular email. Here, access to your mail is not based on your desktop computer – the mail is stored on a remote server. **Hotmail** and **Geocities** are examples.

This means that you can access it at any time from any Net-connected terminal in the world. It doesn't take up any room on your home computer, and you don't even need to own an email application. In fact, you don't need to own a computer. Against this, you only get limited space on the server and your mailbox is smaller. A web-based email account and address are both quite separate from your desktop address; you can't usually access messages from one via the other. Like everything else, though, this may soon be changing.

Features of email programs

Email applications or **email clients** have a variety of standard and automatic features that make them extremely simple and labour-saving to use:

- Your 'Address Book' is a key part of the program. It's the place where you store the email addresses of everyone you communicate with. When someone has emailed you, you can choose to have their address automatically entered under the nickname of your choice. And in programs like Eudora when you want to mail anyone in the address book, you can pull down the 'Send Message to' menu, and click on their nickname; a formatted email appears on your screen. You can also use the address book to store collections of addresses under one nickname. You can even mail out a message to your entire address book, deselecting any individual names.

- When you've composed an email, you can send a copy of it to another person or persons by using the 'cc' (carbon copies) command. If you don't want their addresses to appear on the other copies, you can use the 'bcc' command (blind carbon copies).

- You can automatically reply to an email that you've received without creating a message from scratch. Just pull down the 'Message Menu' and click 'Reply'. Your reply will also include the text of the original message at the bottom, unless you delete it.

- You can 'Forward' on a copy of any email you've received to another person whom you think would be interested. In some programs, you can also 'Redirect' an email, so that the receiver gets it with the original sender's address on it rather than yours.
- You can compose standardized chunks of text called **signatures** to add to any emails. These might include your contact details, greetings, announcements, publicity material, or anything that you may wish to use automatically at will.

Organizing your email messages

The number of messages you receive can build up very quickly. Get into the habit of immediately deleting any you don't need to keep, and organizing the rest. You can keep them as email documents, formatted for your email program, or if you're likely to want to use their content in some other way than as email in the future. You can change them into other application formats by using 'Save As'. Keeping them in email format, you can organize them in a number of different ways:

- Set up 'Auto Sorting' by date, sender or other criteria.
- Set up 'Auto Filtering' by address, subject and so on.
- Set up separate 'Mailboxes' that organize them as they come in, before you read them.
- Organize them yourself by hand into your own system of purpose-made folders (probably the best option).

Sending attachments with email

Buddhists among us may not be too keen on attachments, but for the rest of us they are a terrific adjunct to email. However – and it's a big however – beware of viruses. This topic is covered in some depth on page 59.

You can attach text files, graphic or photo files, web-page files, audio files, music files, video files and more, and the receiver can open them as long as they have the correct software. Some email programs enable you to automatically send other bits and pieces too, such as electronic visiting cards for the receiver to put straight into his or her database.

Attaching files is straightforward – you can usually either use the drop down menu for 'Attach', or drag and drop the attachment's icon onto the email message window.

Talking emails is looking like the next big thing. Voice email technology may not only change personal emailing habits – it is probably going to have a big effect on commercial email publishing. Several companies are already establishing themselves in this field, notably **Bluetooth**. **Talksender (http://www.talksender.com)** is a free piece of software that enables you to use a PC microphone to record up to 60 seconds of voice message for emailing. This is played back when the recipient opens the email, provided they have the software too. This is something you're probably going to be receiving soon from email publishers; voice-enhanced e-junkmail could be coming to a computer near you soon.

Mailing lists

If you're so inclined you can subscribe to any number and variety of special interest emailing lists, in order to be regularly circulated with their material. Some email lists are closed, such as those including only members of a particular organization; others are open. Some are regulated or moderated, while others are much more free-form in their organization. You might want to be discriminating about how many of these you give your email address to; many people find it useful to have one or more 'disposable' free email addresses kept specifically for this purpose. If anything goes wrong and you start to get tons of unwanted email, you can always abandon the address.

To leave a mailing list that you belong to, follow the automatic 'Unsubscribe' option that is usually provided at the bottom of its messages. This is always a different address from the list's regular one for circulation purposes.

When you subscribe to a mailing list, never give anyone the right to pass on your details to anyone else, which is just asking to be spammed (see page 57).

You might even want to start your own emailing list for people who share your particular passion.

Hoax emails

There are lots of hoax emails about these days, and most people don't realize that they are hoaxes. They're getting cleverer all the time. Some of them are just for their own sake, and some are used to collect email addresses by variously playing on your sympathy, compassion, good intentions, greed, fear, guilt or desperation.

They all essentially take the form of the old-fashioned chain letter updated to the electronic age, taking advantage of networks of people who are in touch with each other. They invite you to add your name to the list and then forward the message to everyone in your email address book.

You may be surprised and dismayed to find that some of the most worthy causes you have supported have been the subject of hoax emails. Here are some of the main types:

- A young child in a third world country is dying of a horrible disease and terrible abuse; the XYZ Foundation will donate seven cents to him for every name you can add to the list.
- The women of Afghanistan are being horrendously

oppressed, but adding your name to this petition and forwarding it will really make a difference.

- A certain well-known energizing drink contains a dangerous stimulant which was originally created by the US military to keep soldiers motivated in Vietnam.
- A savage new virus is on the rampage, and you mustn't even think about opening any email that promises you a 'Good Time'.
- Any variation on this: If you forward this email to 20/50/100 people, and send a copy to Nokia/Coca Cola/Microsoft, you will receive a free mobile phone/case of Coke/$1000 dollars from Bill Gates.

Believe it or not, virtually all such tedious chain letters, virus alerts, urban myths, campaign letters and heartbreaking stories are hoaxes. There may be a perfectly genuine and worthy story that has been dragged in, but the promises contained are spurious and deceptive. Before you subject your email contacts to all of this by sending one of these messages on, check out the story on one of the sites that have been set up specially for this purpose, such as:

- **http://www.hoaxkill.com**, or
- **http://www.kumite.com/myths** – the Computer Virus Myths page, or
- **http://www.urbanlegends.com** – the Zeitgeist section of the Urban Legends Archive.

These dedicated sites keep up to date libraries of such material, for the benefit of you and of Net-lore students of the future. They specialize in quick and pain-free debunking. There are however, a few exceptions to this rule – genuine items that are being given a bad name by these hoaxes. One such example is The Hunger Site (**http://www.thehungersite.com**).

Email etiquette

The world of email and its procedures originally evolved spontaneously as a result of individual personal enterprise rather than in any orchestrated way. That's probably why it has developed quite a personal code of conduct – a code of unwritten rules of emailing behaviour, which you'll definitely find it best to stick to. Departing from them not only offends people, it can bring down electronic wrath and bytes of bitter rebuke. At worst, you could end up being cut off by mailing lists, Usenet groups or your ISP. Here are the most important of these generally accepted guidelines. Some are polite gestures, while others are inviolable rules.

- When you receive an important email, try to acknowledge receipt as soon as you can, if a full reply might have to wait for some time. This is because the sender can otherwise not be sure that you've received it.
- When you respond to an email, only leave the original text in the reply message if there's a particular reason

to do so, such as needing the whole conversation preserved for context. If you neglect this, your message
can become a horrible mess of multiple arrow signs
and indented text.

- When you're sending a message to multiple receivers,
  don't make their email addresses public to each other
  without their permission. Achieve this by entering
  them in the 'bcc' address line.

- Files attached to emails can be notoriously slow to
  download. If you intend to send a large file, check with
  the recipient that it is okay to do so, or at least warn
  them. There are few things more annoying than
  opening your email in the morning and finding something that takes half an hour to download and which
  you don't want anyway.

- Never, ever get involved in spamming – using email
  addresses of people you don't know from the circulation lists of messages from others to send unsolicited
  messages. Not even in a small-scale, amateurish way.

- Don't forward any attachments you've received
  without first checking them for viruses.

Other aspects of etiquette that apply to newsgroups and
discussion groups are covered in their respective sections.

Emails and their attachments can carry viruses. See the
advice on viruses on pages 59–62.

4 news, discussion, gossip and chat

Newsgroups and chat rooms are the Web facilities where you can connect interactively with other Net users. Chat rooms have more of a social ambience, while newsgroups or discussion groups emphasize the exchange of information and points of view.

Online news and discussion

Newsgroups and discussion forums represent one of the very oldest services on the Internet. Collectively their part of cyberspace is known as **Usenet**, although other independent discussion groups exist for particular interests within regular websites. Usenet functions like a vast series of bulletin boards, which used to be called BBS, and where anyone can post messages and anyone else can read them. They offer the chance to make contact with other people in an anonymous way, although you can also invite personal replies if you wish. Usenet is the home of free speech on the Web; it's full of people saying more or less anything they please, including some who seem to enjoy being abusive to others. At the same time there's plenty of intelligent conversation, together with the opportunity to obtain very speedy and detailed advice or answers to questions on the subject of your choice. If you post a particular question, you can easily have half a dozen responses within a couple of hours (usually assuming that America is awake).

There are tens of thousands of different newsgroups available, covering almost everything you can think of. As well as these broadly based newsgroups, there are many other discussion groups and forums run within websites, portals and other web communities, that relate to even the most obscure topics, say from dolphin past life therapy to healing with cabbages. However, unsolicited adverts and spamming are increasingly common occurrences with newsgroups these days.

To access newsgroups, you can either visit a web-based interface site that exists for that purpose, or go to the news servers provided by your ISP. The specialized piece of software for accessing newsgroups is the **newsreader**. You can obtain a free web newsreader at Remarq, (**http://www.remarq.com**). You can also configure Microsoft Outlook Express to work as newsgroup access software.

Web-based public news servers include:

- **http://www.freenews.maxbaud.net** – Free Usenet News Servers;
- **http://www.usenetserver.com** – UsenetServer;
- **http://www.newzbot.com** – Newzbot!

It's worth checking how many newsgroups a server carries; unless you're after only certain very specialized subjects, you really want access to about 40,000 in order to make sure that everything significant is covered.

To avoid having to use newsreader software, you can use your browser instead by visiting Deja.com's Usenet Discussion Service at **http://www.deja.com/usenet**. This is generally considered to be the best Usenet archive. You can use it like a search engine, entering subject keywords to get specific messages and to find out which newsgroups include those terms most frequently.

Also check:

- Talkway at **http://www.talkway.com**;
- Supernews at **http://www.supernews.com**; you have to pay US$25 a month, but the news server filters out most of the advertising and spam.

Accessing newsgroups

When you connect to a Usenet facility, you can check the list of groups available, usually in a hierarchy of topics that range from the general to the particular so that you can follow through to a sufficient level of detail to find your particular area of interest. Then you can subscribe to any that appeal to you. Usenet can also be used to transfer attachments, including non-text or **binary** files.

Once you've accessed a group, you can read the postings there. You can do this live while you're online, or download them for reading later while offline. You can then contribute to an ongoing discussion by making your own posting. Or you could start a new **thread** of discussion. There are quite a few matters of security and etiquette that you need to know about when accessing newsgroups.

Newsgroup security

- When configuring your newsreader program or browser for posting to Usenet or any other online group, mask your email address to avoid potential spamming or nuisance email.
- If you do invite personal responses and eventually find that you're receiving unwanted messages from an individual you can use the 'Kill' file to reject mail from that address.

- Virus-check any attached items before downloading or opening, and don't accept any Microsoft Word items with macros.

Newsgroup etiquette

- Upon joining a newsgroup, read any guidelines and **FAQs** that are available as introduction.
- Get a feeling for the discussion rather than hastily joining in. Check the history of a particular thread in order to avoid repeating views that have already been expressed.
- Post only information and views that are relevant to that group.
- Remember that whatever you post is going to be in the public domain. Think your point through before typing it in and read it again before posting.
- Don't post email received from another person unless they sent it to you for that purpose.
- Don't post angry messages. Only use capitals if you really want to convey shouting. Be careful about attracting **flaming** or getting involved in a **flame war**. Watch out for **trolls** – deliberate enticements to start trouble.
- Avoid over-using **smileys** and other **emoticons**.
- Keep your **signature** short and simple.
- Never, ever use the newsgroup for commercial advertisement – unless of course you read a specific request

for someone who channels Hedgehog Wisdom, and that's your bag.

And remember, you can always start your own newsgroup. Maybe on Hedgehog-Wisdom-Channelling.

Chat rooms

Online chat can be extremely compelling and potentially addictive – if you like that sort of thing. It lets you communicate informally with one or more other Net users, often in real time. In other words, you can type in messages and get instant responses before replying again, even if the person you're talking to happens to be on the other side of the world, provided you have the right software.

As well as talking to other people in a chat room, you can use the same kind of facility to ask a celebrity questions in a staged online interview or conference, or chat with friends or relations in other countries without running up massive phone bills.

Themes of chat rooms range from babies to football to healing to money to gossip to technology to sex, and everything in between.

There are several methods of gaining access to online chat:

- Website chat takes place live on an individual site, usually related to the subject of the site or the preferences of the owner. You simply connect to the site's link provided for that purpose, and view the ongoing chat in your browser window. You can key in your own contribution and it will be seen by anyone else viewing that page. See **http://www.talkcity.com**. No extra software is required, but private chat is not necessarily available for some possibilities.
- Celebrity chats are usually moderated by someone who decides whether your question or comment is displayed. BBC TV's chat site, **http://www.chat.beeb.com**, is a good example, with daily visits from the network's stars.
- One-to-one chat and chat with selected individuals is possible with additional **real-time** software such as AOL's **Instant Messenger** or **ICQ** (http://www.icq.com). This is downloaded to your computer from the Net. Instant messengers are essentially a hybridization between email and chat. You can read more about them in the following section.
- If regular text chat seems a bit dull, try 3D chat where users take on a persona and actually walk round chat rooms. More chat connections are listed in the directory section.

Instant messengers. These evolved from regular email, but you allow you to chat instantly with friends or others.

You enter the names of your **buddies** and a control panel tells you when they're online. With some programs you can even talk to them with a microphone and speakers.

Here are some example packages. Generally speaking you have to be using the same program as your buddy. They're all downloadable free.

- AOL Instant Messenger or AIM (**http://www.aol.com**), now in version 4, is probably the most widely used. You don't need to be an AOL subscriber to use it; it will work with any ISP. The sound effects of your buddies coming in and out of the 'room' are cute. If you use AIM, you need to set your preferences to stop people accessing your files.
- Microsoft MSN Messenger (from **http://www.msn.com** or **http://www.msn.co.uk**) is simple to use. Version 4 now integrates with Hotmail.
- Gooey 2.1 (**http://www.gooey.com**) is more like an **Internet Relay Chat** (**IRC**) than an instant messenger. It makes every website you visit a potential chat room.
- Fire Talk (**http://www.firetalk.com**) allows you to enter lots of forums and to teleconference with up to 100 people.
- PowWow (**http://www.tribal.com**) offers text-to-speech facility; when you're in a chat room your computer will read text aloud as it appears in the window.

It will even laugh out loud when it finds the abbreviation **lol**.

Chat room precautions

- Chat software will often ask you for your name and other personal information. Don't feel obliged to register such details, especially if you don't know what they might be used for.
- Remember that whatever people you're chatting to tell you about themselves may or may not be true. The sweet elderly spiritualist you've been conversing with for a year might actually be a nihilist skinhead youth who gets a kick out of kidding people like you along.
- Be very careful indeed if you arrange to meet up with someone you've contacted online; always let someone else know that you're doing so and where you're going.
- Oh yes, and go easy on those smileys.

5 shopping online

Just about any kind of mind-body-spirit goods or services can be bought online, from regular items like crystals and candles and tarot cards, to courses and tuition and holidays, to readings and oracles, and people generally taking over all responsibility from you for running your life, if that's what you want. Spirituality and materialism seem to go hand in hand just fine in this department. Online shopping is probably going to be the leading form of retailing at some point in the future, and it's already grabbing an ever-greater chunk of the market. Books and music have been the leading products in this trend with companies such as Amazon.com famously leading the field, but all kinds of other products are starting to follow suit.

Finding what you want

One option is to shop from individual sites that you already know about, or that you find with a general search engine. But there are also lots of virtual malls these days – collections of shopping websites that may each be based anywhere in the world, but are gathered together in one spot in cyberspace. And there are plenty of these in the mind-body-spirit sector. Then there are specialized search engines serving particular subject areas that may help you to locate your shopping items. And finally, you can find dedicated websites that will automatically scour the whole marketplace for the item you're looking for at the best possible price. This last option tends only to be available for well-known and mass produced goods like fridges and automobiles rather than, say, your one-off fabulazine crystal clusters from Lower Mesopotamia.

Specific search tools and sites are given in the directory, both in the general section and under specific headings.

The thorny issue of shopping security

The single thing that has enabled online shopping to become a reality is your flexible plastic friend, the credit card. You pick the items you want – many sites give you a virtual shopping basket for this – and the total cost is calculated. Then you input your credit card details. And this is the part where we all ask ourselves: should I be worrying about this?

Everyone in the computer business is quick to point out that it's potentially a lot safer to use your plastic in the online realm than in the 'real' world, where people routinely disappear into another room with your card and could be doing anything with it. And overall statistics for credit card fraud seem to back up this observation. Indeed, most web operators are trustworthy and respectable with security arrangements in place to protect your information. Nevertheless there are others who are not to be trusted, and there are trading situations that are not safe, and you have to be able to distinguish between them. Probably a lot more fraud than we realize is taking place; companies don't want to declare information that will undermine their reputation.

There are two main issues at stake here:

1 What happens to your card details when received by the online sales company.
2 What happens to the information when it's on its way to them, passing through many servers along the way.

Some pointers to help you buy with minimum risk:

- Buying with a credit card brings more protection than with a cheque, particularly if an item costs more than £100, and even if you only pay a deposit rather than the full price, because you can claim against the card company if there's a breach of contract with the retailer.
- Be careful where you shop. Wherever possible, buy from well-known and well-established companies. Only shop where there is a full contact address and phone

number; if in doubt, call to check. Keep a record of the transaction, including any reference number.

- Only buy from traders who use an encryption facility to scramble card details in transit. Encryption should at least be up to the standard known as 'secure socket layer', which shows a padlock symbol on screen.

- When buying a very expensive item, look for the highest possible level of encryption and security. You can check a site's **certificate** by clicking 'Properties in IE', or 'View Info' in NS. You can also set browser 'Preferences' to tell you whether a site is considered secure. Bear in mind, though, that 100 percent safety can never be guaranteed.

- Check whether the company has a **privacy statement**, with details of its information handling practice, indicating the uses to which they put information about you. Some companies store personal information on the website rather than on their own facilities, creating a high-risk situation.

- Never send credit card details or other personal information by email.

- You may want to take advantage of packages now offered by insurers for online purchasing, offering protection against fraudulent transactions for an annual premium. Try **http://www.e-shopsafe.co.uk**.

- If you purchase from an e-commerce site that uses **http://www.worldpay.com,** you can arrange purchase insurance through them.

6 you and your website

If you have Internet access, it's very straightforward these days to set up your own website. You may have a business you want to promote; you might want to offer a service; or maybe you just want to convey a bit of your life and personality online so that friends and relatives can find out what's going on with you.

This section gives a short introduction to how to go about this. The directory section lists some sources of further information. The main issues are:

- naming your site;
- where to put it;
- how to design it;
- how to let people know it's there;
- most important, what is it for?

Naming your website

The very first thing to think about is your site name – its domain name. Do this right now. Put this book down, and go see if you can register the name you want now, because it might be available this morning but taken by somebody else by this afternoon.

Domain names and how they work have been introduced on page 28. If your site will be of international interest you might wish to go for a **.com** registration. Otherwise, a national tag such as **.co.uk** may serve better, and give you a greater range of available names. If you're a non-profit or similar organization you can go for **.org**. You might want to register your name with a variety of endings. New codings are likely to be available soon.

- **.com** domain names can be checked at their source, Network Solutions in the US (**http://www.network solutions.com**).
- **.co.uk** domain names are controlled by Nominet (**http://www.nic.uk**.)

You can check with these organizations or with **http://www.register.com** whether the name you want is available. Names are usually bought from domain name resellers, at greatly varying prices, from nothing upwards. When buying from a low-cost provider, check especially fees applying if you want to switch the name from them to a new host.

Where to put it? You also need to think early on about where your site is going to be hosted, and this is often considered in conjunction with buying the name. There are a number of possibilities:

- Most ISPs offer free webspace for this purpose, but then you're going to be stuck with a long and difficult-to-remember domain name given by them rather than chosen by you.
- Alternatively, you can pay an annual fee to the ISP in order to use the name of your choice.
- Better still, you can have your pages hosted on the free webspace, but buy your name from a redirection service that will forward access to your web pages via your name. Freeparking (**http://www.freeparking.com**) is an example of this kind of service.

Designing the site

There are quite a few options for getting this sorted:

- You can call in a professional website builder or design company to build your site, or get a friend to do it. But think about whether they're also going to update it.
- You can purchase one of the many specialized web page

authoring software packages such as **Dreamweaver,**
Adobe Golive, Page Mill, Fusion or, less expensively,
Frontpage 2000, Frontpage is available free, as is
Netscape Composer.

- You can join an online **web community site** that helps
  you design your pages automatically, and can also host
  them for you. This may be particularly useful for specialized subjects or for people who benefit from being
  online alongside others in the same field.

- You can design pages online with sites that specialize in
  this such as **Zyweb** or **Rapid Site**. These usually involve
  payment of a fee, unless you're prepared to accept their
  ads. **Homestead (http://www.homestead.com)** provides this service as well as online accommodation.

- You can use shareware or freeware web authoring programs such as **CoffeCupHTML**, which are downloadable from the Web. See also a useful collection of
  resources at **http://www.Webmonkey.com**

Whichever option you go for, here are some points to
bear in mind:

- First and most important, decide what you want the
  site to do for you and design it accordingly. The best
  attitude to approach this with is realistic-and-hard-
  headed rather than dreamy-and-etheric.

- Visit a lot of sites to see what they're like. Check out

good ones and bad ones in order to work out what makes the difference. There are quite a few websites that list examples of these; some are included in the directory section on page 109.

- Limit the physical size of your pages. Surfers don't like scrolling too far up and down a page.

- Don't use large or high-resolution images that take ages to download. People will get impatient and visit another site rather than wait too long.

- Consider having a very simple and fast-loading front page to your site linking to the other pages, especially if there are many of them.

- Have a clear and well-organized layout for each page and for the whole site.

- Don't overdo special effects. A lot of surfers are annoyed by things that flash excessively, or other such gimmicks – especially if they slow down loading.

- Keep your ego in check. Too much stuff about yourself may not be as interesting to other people as it is to you. Try to imagine what someone who doesn't know you would make of it.

- Before you go public with the site, upload it to the Web; visit it yourself, get other people to visit it, try things out, and get feedback from them. Fix things that need fixing and provide things that are missing and take out things that don't work – or are too naff for

words. Then launch it properly and start telling other
people about it.

- Think of ways in which you can vary and update the
  site to keep it alive. Make it worthwhile to come back
  to.
- If you want to know how many are visiting, install a hit
  counter in the first page. You can get a free one from
  The Counter (http://www.thecounter.com).

Getting your site known

There's not much point in having a site if nobody visits it.
Don't listen to that little inner voice that says to you 'If
you build it, they will come!'; it doesn't work like that.
People you tell directly will know about it, but you probably want others to be able to find out too; this is a key
part of website management. There are a number of
things you can do about it:

- Use correspondence and other publicity you're already
  doing to mention your site. Make it part of your letter-
  head or address labels. Get a sticky label made to
  announce your website address. Launching the site
  could be a good excuse for a PR exercise.
- Add your website URL to your standard email signature. Be careful, though, with seeming to advertise the
  site to people you don't know as this will constitute
  spamming and rightly attract flaming.

- Get your site listed by as many search engines as possible. To do this, give the front page a descriptive title and have meta-tags inserted for appropriate keywords. See **http://www.searchenginewatch.com** for these and other instructions, hints and tips.
- Free submission services such as **Add Engine** (**http://www.addengine.com**) are available for simultaneous submitting to multiple search engines.
- Also submit to web directories, including specialized ones that apply to your field. Examples can be found in the directory section (see page 106). Do searches based on your own keywords to see if these measures are working.
- When you find sites with content that's related to yours, get in touch with the webmasters of those sites by email and suggest exchanging links. This can be automated, with facilities such as **LinkExchange** (**http://www.linkexchange.com**).
- Join an appropriate webring – a group of linked sites that join together to help promote one another. Start with the directory at **WebRing** (**http://www.webring.org**). You'll find other specialized webrings throughout the directory section of this book.

See 'How to Build and Promote an Internet Site' at **http://www.empowermentresources.com/website**.

7 music on the net

Modern developments, MP3 and Napster

Music on the Internet has recently become one of the biggest growth areas, as well as the subject of much controversy concerning copyright infringement. Things that are currently going on with Internet music are probably an indication of what is going to happen with other media such as the content of books, video and multimedia, as the technology moves on and people constantly find new ways of using it.

MP3 technology is what has revolutionized music on the Web – digital audio files that enable music tracks to be sent to and fro, giving CD quality or better upon playback. 'MP3' is the term that is currently most often typed into web searches – more often even than the words 'sex' or 'Pokemon'.

The additional factor that has transformed the potential of MP3 technology is a piece of shareware called

Napster, created by a teenage whizz-kid student in Boston. Napster allows millions of subscribers to pool their music collections on MP3s.

Naturally the music industry is not at all pleased about this development. One person is buying an album and millions of people are copying it for free, instead of the other way round; 25 million songs are estimated as being traded every day at present. The music business reckons that this will cost them billions of pounds a year. And there is no international law prohibiting the copying of music on the Net; the law tends to be about fifteen years behind technology on matters such as this. Individual countries, though, are updating their own legislation; America has already attempted to do so, and the fifteen member states of the European Union are expected to move in this direction soon. But the Internet is borderless, so there will probably be more loopholes than loops for a long time to come.

So the major record companies are desperately launching lots of high-profile lawsuits in an attempt to establish protective precedents, or at least scare some of these operators off. Is this working? Yes and no. People like Napster have been fighting the cases, but others have been seeking ways to become legitimate. MP3.com agreed a settlement with its adversaries. At the same time, everybody is waking up to how attractive these new technologies are, and wanting to get a piece of the action, just as happened with traditional media groups like Time Warner a year or so before. The thinking now is – if you can't beat 'em, join 'em. Both Yahoo and AOL have been talking to online music companies with a view to merger or acquisition. The music onliners have also been talking to music industry giants such as Sony and Seagram. A new player that may become prominent in all this could be the Californian based **http://www.Myplay.com**, which already claims to be operating within the law. It provides a 'virtual locker' which lets users download and play music on any device anywhere in the world. The company claims to pay royalties and police the system's copyright administration. MP3 has reached a royalty agreement with the music publishers, while Napster's actions have been ruled illegal even though, somewhat confusingly, the company has been allowed to continue trading online.

Napster is considered the most rapidly adopted software in the history of the Net so far. Napster can be contacted at **http://www.napster.com**, where free MP3 software is also available. From this site you can choose from a vast range of music and sound files, any of which you can download for free. You just type in the name of an artist or song, and choose from the list of tracks that appears. Downloading currently seems to take anything from ten minutes to half an hour or so. You can then either play the track at will from the MP3 file on your computer, or 'burn' it onto a recordable CD Rom. As well as music there are sound files from such luminaries as The Simpsons, South Park, Star Trek, Monty Python, Star Wars, Woody Allen films or Jerry Seinfeld, to name but a few.

Napster has been faced with a number of major lawsuits and lost some of them, but appears to be moving towards legality through being bought by one of the music industry giants, who all know that they're going to have to embrace this new approach to music technology rather than suppress it. Indeed most commentators feel that peer-to-peer networking is going to be the big thing throughout the internet, and not just in music transfer. An example of this is Gnutella, by which you can access other users' sound files and other kinds of file too; but it isn't currently as easy to use as Napster. Gnutella can be found at **http://gnutella.wego.com** and at **http://www.gnutella.co.uk**.

Some people think the era of commercially recorded disks could be ending before our very eyes. And it's probably only a matter of time before the Net with streaming audio completely eclipses radio as a medium for music and sound.

8 general resources

Before we go into websites that cover more specific topics, let's look at the more versatile web presences that can each lead you to a whole range of other resources. Tools such as search engines and portal sites can be the most crucial of your bookmarks, and will generally have a more lasting presence on the Web, compared with the individual sites that can sometimes come and go in the twinkling of an eye.

Information on ISPs
http://net4nowt.com
http://www.ispreview.co.uk
Directories devoted to free Internet service providers, including lists of unmetered ISPs.

Free software
http://www.shareware.com
For freeware and shareware.

http://www.free-savers.com
http://www.beautifulsavers.com
http://www.desktopsaver.com
Sources of screen-savers.

Online security

http://www.symantec.com
Norton Internet security program for the home PC user.

http://www.alw.nih.gov/Security/prog-full.html
A list of public domain and shareware Internet security software.

http://www.verisign.com
Free security guides that you can download from the digital certificate company VeriSign.

http://www.iss.net
Info about Internet security in general.

http://www.4virus.4anything.com
Links to the best anti-virus software, security specialists and other virus information sites.

Net filtering software

http://www.microsys.com
CyberPatrol.

http://www.pow-dist.co.uk
CyberSitter.

http://www.microtrope.com/icensor.html
Image Censor.

http://www.spyglass.com
SurfWatch.

http://www.shepherd.net
Net Shepherd.

http://www.netnanny.com
Netnanny.

Email sources
http://www.winfiles.com
http://www.download.com
Mac and PC email programs for downloading.

http://www.eudora.com
Eudora's excellent standalone email program, free version
downloadable.

http://www.geocities.com
Free email addresses.

http://www.hoaxkill.com
http://www.kumite.com/myths
http://www.urbanlegends.com
Sites dedicated to unearthing and verifying hoax email material.

Instant messengers

http://www.aol.com
AOL Instant Messenger or AIM.

http://www.msn.com or **http://www.msn.co.uk**
Microsoft MSN Messenger.

http://www.gooey.com
Gooey 2.1 – more like an IRC.

http://www.firetalk.com
Fire Talk – allows you to enter lots of forums and to tele-conference with up to 100 people.

http://www.tribal.com
PowWow – offers text-to-speech facility.

Browser sources

http://www.netscape.com
Netscape browsers.

http://www.microsoft.com.ie
Internet Explorer browsers.

http://www.browsers.com
http://www.browserwatch.com
News, reviews and downloads for a variety of browsers
and operating systems.

http://browsers.evolt.org
Downloadable older versions of browsers for older computers.

Your website
http://www.networksolutions.com
Network Solutions in the US, for checking availability of
.com domain names.

http://www.nic.uk
Nominet, for checking availability of **.co.uk** domain
names.

http://www.register.com
Check whether any name you want is available.

http://www.empowermentresources.com/website
How to build and promote an Internet site.

http://www.microsoft.com/frontpage
Microsoft FrontPage webpage authoring tool.

http://www.adobe.com/prodindex/pagemill
Pagemill web authoring software.

Search engines and directories

http://www.webreference.com/content/search
An in-depth guide to search engines.

http://www.searchengineswatch.com
Up-to-date information on the latest engines, together with hints and tips on using them.

http://www.searchenginewatch.com
http://www.searchenginesgalore.com
For finding specialist sites, check out the specialist engines accessed from here.

http://www.twics.com/-takakuwa/search
Links to engines further afield, from Afghanistan to Zimbabwe.

http://www.super-seek.com
http://www.webdata.com
Lists of directories.

http://www.excite.com/search/
Excite has recently improved its service with Precision Search.

http://www.raging.com
AltaVista's Raging Search.

http://www.alltheweb.com
All The Web directory.

http://www.comparenet.com
http://www.stroud.com, or
http://www.tucows.com
Places to find other search agents.

http://www.yahoo.com
The celebrated Yahoo!

http://www.yahoo.co.uk
Yahoo! UK and Ireland.

http://www.about.com
Experts research and introduce the topics accessed from this site.

Metasearchers and search agents

http://www.google.com

With a new index containing a billion Internet addresses, Google is one of the very best search tools you can use.

http://ask.com
http://ask.co.uk

Ask Jeeves anything at all here.

http://www.copernic.com

Copernic's tool for searching multiple engines and directories.

Specialized search engines

http://www.spiritualsearch.net

Spiritual Search International – a search engine which gathers information and addresses on companies and professionals operating in the spiritual, alternative medicine and environmental sectors of society.

http://www.newhoo.com

NewHoo is a newish search engine with a twist – it's run entirely by Net volunteers, giving something of an anarchic tinge.

'Best-of' website catalogues

http://www.web100.com
Top 100 general websites.

http://www.top50.co.uk/list.htm
Top 50 general UK websites.

http://www.100hot.com
100 hot websites.

http://www.hitbox.com/wc/world.html
Top world 1,000 sites.

http://cool.infi.net
Cool site of the day.

http://www.netsurfcentral.com
Netsurf Central's selection.

There are great numbers of specialized search engines, some built into regular websites and many of which are listed under their particular topics below. Many of the following directories also contain their own search engines.

Mind-body-spirit portals and directories

http://www.dmoz.org

This is one of the most useful of all portals for mind-body-spirit stuff. It has various sub-headings such as Religion and Spirituality or Health/Alternative, each of which leads to hundreds or thousands of links. Use it.

http://www.empowermentresources.com

A terrific access point to all kinds of resources including personal and cultural empowerment, activism, fair trade, environmental awareness, sustainable living and consciousness raising. It has won quite a few website awards. Empowerment seems to be their strongest issue as they lie to the more political end of the mind-body-spirit spectrum.

http://www.newageinfo.com

This is a good portal, and a very comprehensive guide to resources. It has over 200 of its own pages of high quality content, plus links to other authoritative sources. There are quite a few banner ads, though, which you'll probably not want to click on. Its own content is in the nature of basic introductory explanations of the wide range of topics.

http://www.holisticworld.com

A one-stop gateway to some of the best alternative health and mind-body-spirit resources, including both information sites and commercial sites.

http://www.worldtrans.org

A very good entry point to all kinds of individually and globally transformative web stuff – ideas, resources, connections, information and inspiration. It's based in Beverley Hills, California and is maintained by a credit-worthy individual who goes by the name of Flemming Funch.

http://www.globalvisions.org

A spiritual and humanitarian directory with special emphasis on music, arts and media, it has a useful calendar of events and directory of listings as well as links.

http://www.soulhealer.com

Metaphysical and alternative health directory with other resources.

http://www.mindbodysoul.com

A nicely presented portal with connections to check your horoscope, get a tarot reading, track the phases of the moon, find out about business development, discover health products, listen to New Age music and broadcasting. It also promises 'pay per view events', which should be online by the time you read this book.

http://www.wellmedia.com

Tools for a vibrant mind, body and spirit.

http://www.thegarden.net

Portal to a variety of community and globally oriented
ways of using the Net and building Net communities. It
has its own webring, and leads to other webrings.

http://www.spiritweb.org

A big portal site promoting Alternative Spiritual Consciousness, with some very slow-loading pages – perhaps
because they're coming all the way from some Higher
Plane? There's an emphasis on such subject areas as
channeling, lightwork, reincarnation, mysticism and UFO
sightings. It claims to be the oldest and largest directory
of its kind on the Web, with 28 million page views to date.

http://www.newagecities.com

A broadly based and commercially oriented portal site whose front page prominently offers online connection to psychics, as well as inspiration for 'when all you wanted isn't enough'.

http://www.accessnewage.com

One of the most comprehensive providers of links to all things new-agey.

Webrings

There are very many webrings on the Internet, some of which are listed below under their topic. To get direct access to many of them, go to **http://www.webring.org/what**

Discussion and newsgroups

There are a great number of Usenet newsgroups that offer discussion on mind-body-spirit topics. Again, many of these are listed under their respective headings below. Below are some more general groups and sources.

http://www.egroups.com

A generic starting point for discussion groups.

http://www.remarq.com

Obtain a free web newsreader at Remarq, for accessing newsgroups.

http://www.deja.com/usenet
http://www.talkway.com
http://www.supernews.com
Usenet discussion services.

http://www.freenews.maxbaud.net
http://www.usenetserver.com
http://www.newzbot.com
These are web-based public news servers.

http://www.lightandlife.com
Light and Life Journal. 'A gathering place for truth seekers of all types'.

http://www.namee.com
Oz's New Age site for discussion, chat, bulletins, personal ads and so on.

http://www.clubs.yahoo.com/clubs/emergingawareness
Emerging awareness discussion groups at Yahoo.

Usenet discussion groups related to alternative health and related topics:

- alt.folklore.aromatherapy
- alt.folklore.herbs
- alt.healing.flower-essence

- alt.healing.reiki
- alt.health.ayurveda
- alt.health.dental-amalgam
- alt.health.oxygen-therapy
- alt.meditation
- alt.meditation.moderated
- alt.meditation.qigong
- alt.meditation.quanyin
- alt.meditation.shabda
- alt.meditation.transcendental
- alt.philosophy.taoism
- alt.philosophy.zen
- alt.psychology.transpersonal
- alt.recovery
- alt.recovery.aa
- alt.recovery.addiction.sexual
- alt.recovery.adult-children
- alt.recovery.codependency
- alt.recovery.compulsive-eat
- alt.recovery.na
- alt.recovery.religion
- alt.recovery.sexual-addiction
- alt.religion.buddhism.tibetan
- alt.religion.eckankar
- alt.support.asthma.buteyko
- alt.yoga
- alt.zen

- misc.health.alternative
- rec.food.veg
- rec.food.veg.cooking
- sci.life-extension
- sci.med.midwifery
- sci.med.nutrition
- talk.environment

These can only be reached by using a 'newsgroup reader' (see page 78) as they are not the normal html pages that can be directly reached by using a browser. Some browsers do, however, incorporate a newsgroup reader option (e.g. Outlook Express).

http://www.liszt.com/select/Culture/New_Age
http://www.spiritweb.org/Spirit/mailing-lists.html
Online mailing and discussion lists.

Access to many others can be found within specific websites listed under their respective topics.

Shopping sites

There are unlimited mind-body-spirit shopping opportunities on the Web. You can buy goods, services, books, music, holidays and a whole lot more. A great number of these facilities will be found on the sites listed under their subject headings below. Here are just some of the more generic shopping sites, including some that cater for a broad range of products and services. Make sure you take the security precautions described on page 87.

http://www.dmoz.org/Shopping/Health_and_Beauty/Alternatives

You'll find a massive 1387 direct shopping links from this Open Directory site, under product and service headings such as aromatherapy, flower essences, herbs, books or even oxygen (we have to pay for it now?). Plus a whole series of individual links to businesses that specialize in particular products such as wild foods, magnets, Zen Fountains, apricot kernels, porcupine quills, cat's claw, shark cartilage, kava kava, deer velvet, seaweed, holistic pet shampoos, emu oil and purchases based on guidance in the scriptures. (We didn't make up any of these).

http://www.ethical-junction.org

Access to a vast array of ethical goods and services from a wide range of companies. The site organizers check the core activities of their subscribing companies against the site's ethical criteria. Visitors can check on this information before buying.

http://www.ecomall.com

Somewhat basic in design, this fully searchable site nevertheless has a huge number of green-related shopping links, and a set of articles on environmental issues.

http://www.matoska.com

An attractive and very extensive online shop specializing in Native American related products including books, music, videos, beads, bells, shells, feathers, leather and more.

http://www.empowermentstore.com

A huge website that is halfway between an environmental shop and an Internet portal. Rather busy in design, it offers a search engine that will compare the prices of green products that can be purchased online.

http://www.fourwinds-trading.com

Another highly attractive and well designed site offering traditional Native American products such as books, music and video.

http://www.mindbodysoul.com

A huge marketplace portal for all kinds of mind-body-spirit shopping online.

http://www.mindbodyspirit.net

Online store for stuff like crystals, tarot, aromatherapy products, books etc.

http://www.newageinfo.com/products.htm

Links for product New Age companies.

http://www.thinknatural.com
Alternative remedies and beauty products.

http://www.healthshop.com
A very big site, which also has lots of health data, quizzes, polls and stuff like that.

http://www.healthtree.com
Budget health supplements direct. Not very holistic.

http://www.sheilanproductions.com
New Age gifts and information.

http://www.greenseal.org
Access to the Global Eco-labelling Network for validating ecological credentials.

http://www.uniquelyglobal.com
A selection of gifts that have been hand-picked from around the world.

http://www.gossypium.co.uk
Now here's a good idea – an online clothes service that brings together organic cotton farmers in India with ethi-cally minded consumers (in Britain only, at present). The beauty of it is that you can customize your clothes at a click of your mouse, and they're made to order. Why don't

you log on from the US and see if you can get the service too?

Books

Books are available from most of the generic online shops as well as from very many sites listed in the subject directory. Here are some sites that specialize in the bookish end of things.

If you're buying books online, bear in mind that you can help many of your favourite sites by buying through their facilities from people like Amazon.com. The site gets a commission that can range from five percent to 15 percent, and it doesn't cost you any more. Many .org or non-profit sites rely on this form of revenue to be able to stay in business and offer their very valuable services.

http://www.addall.com
http://www.bestbookbuys.com
http://www.isbn.nu
Search engines that compare book prices.

http://www.thorsons.com
The website of the mind-body-spirit arm of HarperCollins, which offers much more than just books. You can consult on astrology, explore aspects of personal development, parenting, tantric sex, yoga and many aspects of

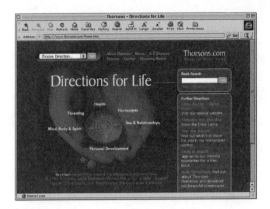

mind-body-spirit. You can also sign up for an email
newsletter and order books online if within Europe.

http://www.eastwest.com
Over 35,000 books available.

http://www.nowbooks.co.uk
Online ordering for international esoteric publishers such
as Bear and Co and Celestial Arts. For 'serious spiritual
journeyers'.

http://www.clever.net/lifequest/bookshop
New Age wholesale directory. Books plus video, audio,
clip-art and other new-agey things.

http://www.taobooks.com

Also has music, tapes, gifts, posters and remedies.

http://www.ZenTeabags.com

Many humorous books from Gerry Maguire Thompson about mind-body-spirit stuff and the human condition in general, such as the spiritually uplifting 'Conversations with Dog'.

http://www.chopra.com

The extensive website of the alternative medicine practitioner and very popular guru figure includes a 'quote of the day', a 'recipe of the week' (vegan and vegetarian), 'spiritual law of the day' (not to be confused with the 'seasonal dharma' or the 'question of the day') as well as an email community, links and a collection of articles.

http://www.marsvenus.com

The world of John Gray. The best-selling bookwares of the author of *Men are from Mars, Women are from Venus*.

http://www.empowermentbooks.com

The book section of the empowerment store is worth an entry in its own right for its articles and resources, particularly in its health categories.

Audio and video

A number of sites such as those listed here specialize exclusively in audio content. You'll find more sources elsewhere in these pages, especially under 'shopping'.

http://www.bigsurtapes.com

An interesting American online store offering spoken word tapes of 'some of the most innovative and visionary thinkers of this century'. There are no opportunities to preview any such material from the site, though, which is a shame.

http://www.innergear.com

Expensive subliminal programming tapes are available to buy online from this site.

http://www.lightworksav.com

An extensive online store offering videos (in European as well as US format) and audio tapes on a wide range of mind-body-spirit subjects. 'America's premier distributor of empowering media', it says.

http://www.newagetalk.com

A free Internet talk radio station promising interviews, celebrity guests, live concerts, educational programming and 'much more'.

http://www.broadcast.com/audiobooks
Yahoo's audio books on a variety of topics including self-help.

http://www.audiosource.com
New Age and self-help audio books.

http://www.stoneclave.com/broadcast
The Candle – 'cyberadio for the soul'.

Magazines

The World Wide Web contains many sites that constitute both online magazines and a web presence for print magazines. Here is a selection that includes both. Many more print and online magazines are mentioned under their respective subject headings.

http://www.omnimag.com
The online presence of the now suspended *OMNI* magazine still offers a wide range of interesting links and facts, but you must grapple with an unusual and confusing navigational design. Includes online fiction and a set of simple 'mind-brain' tests.

http://www.conscious-living.com.au
The website of Australia's 'leading health and lifestyle magazine' includes a very extensive holistic resource directory.

http://www.magicalblend.com
The website of the magazine that offers 'an entertaining and thoroughly unique look at the modern spiritual lifestyle'. The website apparently only has a small amount of the magazine's content, although you may subscribe to its email newsletter.

http://www.utne.com
The *Utne Reader* – just about the best magazine you could read, because it includes the best bits of the other magazines.

http://www.newage.com
New Age – one of the most successful print magazines for commercial coverage of the New Age.

http://www.ru.org
New Renaissance – a journal for spiritual awakening.

http://www.peacezine.org
A peace newsletter.

<u>Music</u>

The latest music developments on the Net have been described on pages 97–100. Here is a selection of sites that specialize in mind-body-spirit type music content.

http://www.newagemusic.com/links.html

This links page from a website dedicated to servicing the New Age music industry is well worth a look. It's not the most organized list, but it is extensive and wide-ranging.

http://www.silverwave.com

A good music site for own label and artists, coming out of Boulder, Colorado; it's been going for 14 years. The site includes world music, native American music and music of the seasons. You can try the sound samplers or get information on the artists, new releases or concerts and events.

http://www.globalvisions.org

Artists and titles such as Suxanne Teng, Mystic Journey, Donovan, Wind Spirit, James Durst and Alex Wilding. You

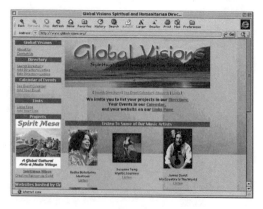

can sample these online if you have the plug-ins (see pages 43–4).

http://www.worldmusicportal.com
Like the name says, and searchable. A simple design holds a lot of information about various world artists – the list is not exhaustive, but this is a nice site without overbearing commercialism, or an online store in sight.

http://www.newagesound.com
A well designed commercial website specializing in a fairly small but select number of artists. An online listening post is available for you to try before you buy.

http://www.putamayo.com
An attractively simple design for this online store specializing in world music. It supplies lots of information about its artists.

http://www.alula.com
The website of a record company specializing in 'contemporary world music, Celtic, and Americana'; MP3s are available for free download, so you can try before you buy in the online cyberstore.

http://www.backroadsmusic.com
New Age and ambient music catalogue.

http://www.Nativeamericanmusic.com
A site that specializes in Native American music.

http://www.hyperreal.com
A definitive list of ambient music and drug culture. Far out man.

http://www.planet-e-music.com
Extensive catalogue of New Age music.

http://www.audiocollage.com
Stress reduction music on CD or cassette.

http://www.alt.music.world
Newsgroup on world music.

Napster replacements
http://www.mp3.com
Pay-and-play MP3s.

http://www.listen.com
Search here for downloadable music.

http://www.scour.com
Scour daily downloads here, for music and other types of software. Like Napster, Scour is currently being 'legalized'.

http://www.emusic.com/promo/yahoo/
Free MP3-a-day.

http://www.tapster.com
Spinal Tap rules! From the legendary spoof rockumentary.

Travel, holidays, courses and events

The Internet provides perhaps the best possible way to find out about activities, whether locally or globally. Here are some links to start you on your journey.

http://www.powerplaces.com
Trips to sacred destinations with leading facilitators.

http://www.piedmontyoga.com
Yoga holidays in the USA.

http://www.freespirituk.com
Free Spirit Travel – activity holidays in Europe.

http://www.skyros.com
Long-established Greek holiday outfit, which now also offers mind-body-spirit activity holidays in the Bahamas and other parts of the world.

http://www.cortijo-romero.co.uk
Mind-body-spirit activity holidays in Spain.

http://www.Vegiventures.com
Vegetarian holidays.

http://www.esalen.com
Esalen Institute – the ultimate Californian transformation centre, with a legendary program.

http://www.findhorn.org
Famous pioneering community in Scotland with a full program of events, including major conferences.

Games

The games that you can play or obtain online make a whole world of their own; there seem to be people who live, breathe, eat and sleep these games. The vast majority of games are about wars, battles, fighting, carnage, death, destruction and mayhem, or at least racing or other form of competition. There are some exceptions, however. Some of the simulation games or **sims** have an ecological basis, involving creation of cities, countries or ecologies. Here are some general sites for finding games and game related information, plus a selection of more mind-body-spirit oriented games that can be found online.

http://www.opensorcery.net
This subversive site makes use of something called a **games patch** – a hacked piece of code that subverts a

commercially available computer game such as Quake or Tomb Raider, enabling it to be manipulated, changing the characters or altering the experience of the game. The most famous was Nude Raider, no longer available for legal reasons. But Open Sorcery has links to more subversive patches still, that radically alter games to promote an agenda of their own, including feminism.

http://www.messiah.com
Download a demo of this unusual game from here: you play Bob, a working-class angel ordered by God himself to go and clean up the putrid, disgusting, sleazy, and infested world of the future.

http://www.entrepreneurs.net/clm/kindgame
The Kindness Game.

http://www.gamecenter.com
Part of the CNET service, this is the place to come to for downloads of current popular games. Not a website with a mind-body-spirit emphasis, but there are several genres of games to choose from, so you might find something a bit like 'Ecco the Dolphin' here, if you're lucky.

http://www.oglibrary.com
This is a tremendous resource for anyone interested in online gaming of any kind – from fantasy RPGs to chess.

A very nice design, with informative sub-directories: highly recommended.

http://www.totalgames.net

A website dedicated to reviews and hints and tips for popular commercial console and computer games.

http://www.generosity.org

The generosity game involves doing nice things for total strangers and leaving behind a plastic card saying so. Can it catch on and become the chain letter of the 21st century? Find out more from the website.

http://www.theatreduplicity.co.uk

MindShare – a new and exciting game from Eliza Wyatt that is absorbing, transformative and fun. It turns on all the games we ourselves play in life, like 'being right' or 'being victim'. Highly recommended. You can also email **elitinay@aol.com**

http://www.worldtrans.org/pos/infinitegames.html

A 'vision of life as play and possibility'.

mind

In this section we've included websites that relate to mentally oriented activities, such as attitudinal training or personal training, meditation or dreamwork, as well as mind therapies; plus all the major forms of oracle or divination. In this latter category, topics such as Feng Shui and a vast range of different kinds of astrology are among the strongest presences on the World Wide Web.

There's certainly no shortage of astrology sites on the Web. Many of them are personality led websites from such wonderfully named individuals as Astrobella, DeeAstro and SpiritWyse. Some sites give you readings, others tell you how to astrologize yourself. As well as the different world astrologies they cover all kinds of other species such as medical astrology, financial astrology, love astrology, astrological cookery, astrological numerology and soul-centre astrology. You name it, somebody does astrology for it.

Another large web presence is sites that focus on developing positivity in one way or another. It's long been recognized that there is power in developing our attitude and way of thinking in order to transform our experience of life for the better, and this has become a key part of the mind-body-spirit movement. This approach began to be an influence on mainstream culture in the 1950s with people such as Dale Carnegie and books like *The Power of Positive Thinking* and *How to Win Friends and Influence People*. The same principles were enthusiastically taken up and developed by the business and corporate world, especially in the field of sales. Now the whole thing is developing in a much more holistic direction, and there's a lot of it out there on the Web. Some of these sites represent those relentless-optimism-no-matter-what options that can be such a pain in the butt, but others contain good constructive, realistic or inspiring stuff. Listed in this guide are some of the better sites and resources for you to check out.

As we all know, most of the world's media thinks we're only interested in hearing bad news, which undeniably holds an incredible fascination for most of us. Good news is rarely considered newsworthy by the major conventional media. But now there is a whole new genre of organizations that transcend this tendency, with their newspapers, magazines, radio and TV channels. It's a big growth area. Most of them now have web presences too.

There are also a lot of psychics out there on the Net – and some people who think they're psychic. It's one of those commodities that seems to be particularly prolific online, so just a few are listed. When I visited the 'psychic' area of New Age Web Works (**http://www.newagewebworks.com**), 'for the most accurate psychic readings on the Net', I got a notice saying 'Our Psychic area is Temporarily Out of Service'. You'd think they'd have seen it coming!

9 mind training

The whole field of personal coaching, motivational training and self-improvement is pretty big on the Web,
undoubtedly because these phenomena have been prominent for decades in North America. These days it often
seems to be done over the phone, with coaches helping
clients on opposite sides of the Atlantic (or the planet).

Coaching

Personal coaching has become very big in the last few
years, spreading from the US to Europe and elsewhere.
Here are some leads from different areas.

One of the best starting points for web resources is to go
to **http://www.dmoz.org/Health/Alternative/Coaching**
where you will find 122 links at the last count.

http://www.personalbreakthrough.com
This is worth a look; articles are invited from anyone on

anything related to the subject that they feel strongly about or have expertise in.

http://www.sedonamethod.com
This is an approach that focuses on dealing with emotions. The man who invented it sounds like a rather wonderful human being. There is lots of explanatory stuff on this site.

http://www.lifementoring.com
Personal development in a friendly community.

http://www.coachreferral.com
A referral system to find personal coaches.

Motivational training

http://www.mindmedia.com
Mind Media Life Enhancement Network – a communal site selling 'mindware' online, interactive mind-, self- and personality-improving stuff. Perhaps more importantly, it's a very useful and well organized portal to a great number of links that spread over this whole field.

http://www.self-worth.com
'Home of the Motivational Mailer' – encouragement sent free to your email inbox. Essentially a set of testimonials from people who have overcome hardship or misfortune,

organized into categories: cyberchicken soup for the online soul.

http://www.dreamlife.com
The giant of personal training, Tony Robbins' self-improvement website.

http://www.selfgrowth.com
David and Michelle Riklen's webguide. Boasts access to over 4,000 sites for self-improvement.

http://www.netseminar.com
A site for finding self-improvement and other educational seminar in your area.

Personal development
http://www.transformation.org
A slickly designed website, the main feature of which is an online self-awareness survey (SAS). Underlying the free basic membership is a substantial push for the organization's products and services, which cost rather a lot.

http://www.dreamhuge.com
A large and attractive website dedicated to 'inspiring people to live their dreams'. Topics are very well cross-referenced and although you may choose to buy from here, selling is not the only purpose to these pages.

http://www.ansir.com

I took Ansir's online personality test, which is massive and took ages; but then twice had to answer 'tie-breakers' to discover my personality type. The end of all this was my set of seven 'keys', which didn't enlighten. Good-looking site though.

http://www.ZenTeabags.com

Personal transformation through comedy. This site emanates from the author of this book, who runs workshops on this topic worldwide.

http://www.living-software.com

Option Institute personal growth programs for health, happiness and success, based on the work of Barry Neil Kaufman.

http://www.seminarmaster.com

One-stop shopping for seminars and workshops in all parts of the US.

http://www.keirsey.com

Allows you to find out your temperament type online. Are you, for instance, the kind of person who consults the Internet to find out what kind of person you are?

http://www.comngrnd.com

Common Ground quarterly journal online – 25 years of articles from this legendary San Francisco Bay area publication – plus 700 listings and other resources.

http://www.ethos.com

Radio: The Ethos Channel. Online streaming media, featuring content from top self-improvement figures.

10 positivity

http://www.worldtrans.org/positive.html

This portal-style site is one of the best entry points for
this whole subject area, leading you along many other
pathways into related zones and topics. It's refreshingly
non-commercial in its content and discriminating choice
of who to be linked with. The site dedicates itself to all

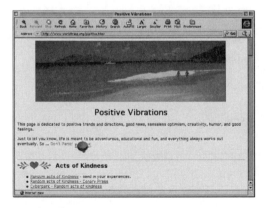

kinds of positive trends and directions, good news, optimism, creativity and humour. The 'Random Acts of Kindness' link is one of the most interesting.

http://www.positiveprojections.com
We found this website rather irritating, but it is dedicated to the power of positive thinking as advocated by the effusive and endearingly positive Diana Brock.

http://www.mindport.net/~niceones
The Nice Ones – 'an organized fellowship of good people'.

http://www.option.org
The Option Institute. These folks' business is teaching people how to live happier, more comfortable and successful lives. Sounds good.

http://www.positive-place.com
'A Positive Place on the Internet'.

Positive New Media

http://www.oneweb.com/goodnews
The *Optimist* – a 'good news' newspaper.

http://www.PositiveNews.com
The groundbreaking UK based newspaper, with global content. Their entire archive is going online.

http://www.upbeat.net
Another 'positive news' vehicle.

http://www.alt.goodnews
http://www.alt.society.kindness
Positive newsgroups and message boards.

http://www.worldtrans.org/pos/forum
A 'positive vibrations forum'.

Inspiration

http://www.chickensoup.com
Chicken Soup for the Soul. This site is not about Jewish cooking.

http://www.inspire.org
Inspirational exercises and instruction.

http://www.y-knot.com
The power of 'why not'. Cute URL. And why not?

http://www.inspirationalstories.com
After-hours inspirational stories, plus jokes, poems, quotes ...

http://www.heartwarmers4u.com
Sends you inspirational emails daily, as well as providing access to a lot of sites.

http://www.eur.nl/fsw/research/happiness
World Database of Happiness.

http://www.halcyon.bizland.com
The Illuminated Message Board. Find or leave an inspirational message, question, insight or story about experience of life.

Mind machines

http://www.dream-world.com
Mind machines and related info, including books and audio.

http://www.cerebrex.com
Distributor of mind machines as well as psycho-acoustic soundscapes, ionisers etc.

These are just a few examples of the myriad commercial sites on this subject. For more sources, see many of the retail sites listed under Shopping (page 116).

Stresswork

http://www.stressless.com
Site selling stress related products and programs. To reduce it, that is.

http://www.calmcentre.com

Sound de-stressing info online from Paul Wilson, the author of the *Little Book of Calm*, the *Big Book of Calm*, the *Book of Calm for Goldfish* and many other books of calm.

http://www.happiness.co.uk

Become a smilier happier person with this influential UK-based organization.

Creativity

http://www.creativity.net

The Creativity Cafe describes itself as a transformational theatre and networking salon, a new school for the next millennium, creating art and technology for a better world. They're relative online old-timers, having been 'netcasting' since 1994. They are there to facilitate creative expression, with focus on theatre, music and the arts. The site boasts such items as a community noticeboard, a mailing list of artists who are using technology for humanity, courses in digital storytelling, a Maui artists' showcase, and 'living gallery' events – live online art showcases for the audience's inspiration and networking; plus lots of links to kindred-spirited sites. There are also some more inscrutable items such as spirit body photography and a bewildering link offering free ChromaDepth 3D glasses that your dog can also wear.

http://www.bemorecreative.com

A directory of creativity links and inspirational creative quotations.

http://www.aptt.com

Unmemorable URL for Edward de Bono, the granddaddy of lateral thinking. Online resources for creativity training, thinking skills, innovation tools and attention skills plus training workshops and seminars.

http://www.enchantedmind.com

Enchanting address for this fund of techniques and resources on creativity.

Or you could be even more creative and build your own creativity website.

11 mindstates

Meditation

What better entry point could you choose than **http://www.dmoz.org/Religion_and_Spirituality/meditation**, which has a mighty 169 links?

http://www.alt.meditation
Meditation newsgroup and discussion.

http://www.alt.meditation.transcendental
Transcendental Meditation newsgroup.

(See also Buddhism for more sites on this subject, page 216).

Dreamwork
http://www.lucidity.com
The Lucidity Institute – how to have a lucid dream – one where you realize that you're dreaming, and can sometimes consciously change the content.

http://www.members.xoom/com/howtodream
Lucid dreaming and dreaming links library. A collection of the 'best' dream sites on the Net. A dream of a site?

http://www.spiritweb.org/Spirit/lucid-dreaming.html
Lucid dreaming links.

http://www.dreamup.com
Your very own dream analysis and dream journal assistant.

http://www.dreamed.com
Interactive dreaming. Offers a multimedia CD, including dreamwork and dream journal database.

http://www.alt.dreams
Dream newsgroup and discussion.

http://www.TheAgeofMeaning.com
Discussion group on dream interpretation.

http://www.alt.dreams.castaneda
Discussion about dreams from the perspective of the work of Carlos Castaneda, the celebrated author of South American shamanism books.

12 mind helpers

Psychics

http://www.singingpsychic.com

Is this a spoof site? Apparently not; it's a simple but rather endearing site that publicizes Texan Fran Baskerville – famed psychic, ghostbuster and detective. Apparently Fran has repeatedly won the World's Greatest

Psychic Award over the past ten years. She's found over 5,000 missing persons and predicted on TV and radio the deaths of JFK and Princess Diana. Most intriguingly, she discovered her psychic abilities after a Near Death Experience involving an eighteen wheel lumber truck. Fran's latest CD includes the track, 'The Grassy Knoll', from an eyewitness account of Mr Kennedy's assassination. And she sings your readings. Unfortunately you don't get them online, you have to call her.

http://www.newagecities.com
Offers online connection to live psychics whom you can see, hear and chat to for a fee, with different consultants at various weekly time slots.

http://www.awakenone.freeservers.com
Resources and instruction for your own psychic development.

With intuition, you'll be able to find a whole lot more psychic sites out there.

Counselling and psychotherapy

http://www.cyberpsych.com
This is the infrequently updated site of Robert F. Sarmiento, Ph.D., a psychologist from Houston, Texas. It contains a number of essays on subjects such as depression, anxiety, career and relationship issues.

http://www.metatalk.com
Free personal counselling, focusing on growth and rebirth.

http://www.docinthebox.com
Calvin J. Langmade's psychological counselling online.

http://www.mental-health-matters.com
Yes, it does. An information and resource directory.

http://www.isyke.com
This site offers facilities for therapists to set up practice online.

http://www.shrinksonline.com
A virtual community, for psychology professionals only.

<u>Hypnotherapy</u>

http://www.dmoz.org/Health/Alternative/Hypnotherapy
A very useful resource of 234 links on hypnotherapy and related topics.

http://www.hypnosis.ac
Hypnotherapy tapes for losing weight, quitting smoking, pain-free childbirth and other addictions/phobias.

http://www.positivechanges.com
A franchise of US hypnotherapy centres.

http://www.TranceWorks.com
Books on hypnotherapy and related subjects.

http://www.selfhypnosis.com
Free online audio training in relaxation, meditation and self hypnosis. Programme yourself to remember to log off when you've finished ...

http://www.alt.hypnosis
Discussion and newsgroup on hypnosis and hypnotherapy.

Neuro-Linguistic Programming (NLP)

http://home.earthlink.net/~jbodnar/nlp.html
A really good selection of links to start from.

http://www.nlpinfo.com/
Good introductory site and resources.

http://www.nlpresources.com/
Excellent NLP site.

http://www.nlp.org/
A comprehensive if commercial site with extensive links and resources.

http://www.purenlp.com/
A commercial site but with a huge list of 'cool links'.

http://www.rain.org/~da5e/nlpfaq.html
Excellent FAQs on NLP and the home of the alt.psychology.NLP newsgroup.

http://www.worldbeststudy.com.au/poweroff.html
Brian Clarke's article on the 'ultimate success formula'.

Creative visualization
http://www.goalmaker.com/links.asp
A good set of links from a website that offers goal-making software for trial download.

http://www.paragongeneration.co.za/tips/tips14.html
Tips on creative visualization from this South African site.

http://www.calstatela.edu/faculty/nthomas/
An interesting website maintained by Nigel Thomas, a Californian academic with research interests in imagination, mental imagery and consciousness.

New physics
New physics has now come to embody much ancient wisdom such as the principles of Buddhism, the physical workings of life, the universe and everything. Check out these examples.

http://www.magna.com.au/~prfbrown/capra_0.html
The web publication of the 8th chapter of Fritjof Capra's 'Turning Point'. Capra was the author of the groundbreaking *The Tao of Physics*.

http://www.angelfire.com/md/glaucon/physics.html
An article considering the domain of the sciences through modern physics.

http://www.virtualchaos.org
The 'superstrings' theory of everything.

13. oracles and divination

http://www.dmoz.org/ReligionandSpirituality/Divination
Open Directory Project's massive 1,503 links on a variety
of divinatory topics.

http://www.aquarianage.org
A large and interactive site covering oracles, divination

and astrology as well as other 'New Age' beliefs. There's lots of stuff for you to try, to learn how to do, and of course to buy (I could have predicted that). However, the site is riddled with adverts, including products not normally associated with mind-body-spirit such as diet coke. Hence not recommended.

Astrology

http://www.spiritweb.org/Spirit/astrology
Useful portal for astrological resources of all kinds. Has direct links on astrology basics, Western astrology and Vedic astrology, plus astrological FAQs. Then there's a discussion forum where you can follow topics such as 'Is Libra a positive or negative sign?' or 'Sad Sagittarian seeking guidance'. Plus 635 other links to assorted astrological websites. Seems to be very slow-loading.

http://www.astro-psychology.com
Includes an online counselling service.

http://www.alt.astrology
Astrology discussion and newsgroup.

Western zodiac astrology

http://www.astrology.org
With a reputation for fun, this site offers free soul mate matching and both daily and weekly predictions for all

areas of your life. Plus you can order your own birth chart and discover which star signs make the best crystal healers or used-car salesmen.

http://stars.metawire.com
Another popular and fun site, with horoscopes for the day, the week or the year; and useful stuff on compatibility, from the highly rated (in terms of tabloid horoscopes, anyway) Jonathan Cainer.

http://www.astrobaby.com
A good idea – an astro-site that completely dotes on babies with mini-charts, babyscopes, birth charts, announcements and guess what – lots of gift ideas! But can they help you deal with post-natal depression?

http://www.astrologyobserved.com
This has been described as 'an astrology site for grown-ups', with an astrological 'weather forecast' for everyone, rather than just for sun signs.

http://www.yourastrologysite.com
Free personal daily horoscopes based on your birth date.

http://www.astrologer.com
Another comprehensive astrology site.

http://www.prodigy.com
Gynme Mayer pages – astrology and karmic understanding.

http://www.astroecon.com
Economics and stock market forecasts. Perhaps useful for planning your ethical investment moves.

http://www.theastrologycookbook.com
Tasty stuff!

http://www.astrology-numerology.com
Astrological numerology. Or is it numerological astrology?

Astrological software

http://www.astrograph.com
Interactive astrological software for both Mac and Windows computers.

http://www.ceze.com/astro
Databases in English, French and German for localities and time zones; transits, synastries, progressions, sun and moon returns – it's all here, with graphics and interpretation.

http://www.world-of-wisdom.com
Astrology software items that include Horoscope Interpreter, Astrology for Lovers, as well as basic information about astrology and monthly horoscopes.

http://www.goravani.com

Astrological software for Vedic astrology, plus down-loadable training videos and demonstration software complete with Sanskrit pronunciation sound files.

Chinese astrology

http://www.chineseastrology.com

Chinese Astrology by Shelly Wu. 'Modern interpretation of ancient wisdoms.'

http://www.chineseastrologyonline.com

Free information on dating, marriage, compatibility and lucky times and places.

http://www.chinese-astrology.com

Horoscopes, energy tracker, and fortune cookies too.

http://www.chinesefortunecalendar.com

Information is adapted to US time zones. A bonus is that you can get help in picking a fortunate name for a newborn baby. Astrobella or Spiritwyse, perhaps?

Hindu or Vedic astrology

Indian Hindu Vedic or Jyotish astrology is surprisingly well covered on the Web. Here is a sample selection of sites.

http://www.newageinfo.com/vedic
A very good introduction to the subject – simple and easy to understand, yet also with some depth.

http://www.vedanet.com
American Institute of Vedic Studies. Correspondence courses on Vedic astrology.

http://www.astrology-india.com
The Astrological Society of India offers services in traditional Indian horoscopes, marriage compatibility and annual forecasts.

http://www.bava.org
The British Association for Vedic Astrology: a European forum for Vedic astrology, including arranging of meetings and conferences.

Other astrologies

http://www.members.aol.com/anistatia
World Astrology – a forum for applying and combining Chinese, Tibetan, Vedic, Arabian, Judaic and western astrologies in daily life.

http://www.tbgraphic.com/zodiac
An interactive site about Vietnamese astrology.

http://www.jonsandifer.com
British author and expert on Nine Star Ki or Feng Shui astrology.

http://www.secretcycles.com.au
Astro palmistry: Hindu palmistry and Vedic astrology for events in life. Promises 'actual dates of occurrences'. Do you really want to know?

I Ching

http://www.iching.com
Oracle of Change – a multimedia version of the ancient and venerated oracle of throwing the sticks and finding strategies for life situations.

http://www.pacificcoast.net/~wh/index
A huge number of I-Ching-related links are available here, including several to online versions of the oracle, plus commentaries and translations.

http://www.visionarynet.com
Online I Ching readings, in modern language.

http://www.Iching.com
I Ching readings with emphasis on usefulness.

Runes

http://tarahill.com/runes/

A nice starting point for the online exploration of runes and their meanings.

http://members.aol.com/cbsunny/

Another good resource for the research of the 'alphabet of mystery'.

http://www.newageinfo.com/res/asatru

This fine site about Norse spirituality has content and links on runes.

http://www.irminsul.org/ru/ru.html

A really good collection of links and resources. Includes runic fonts and downloadable rune casting programs.

http://www.earth-dancing.com/runes.htm

An interesting site, chiefly concerning Nordic versions of the runes.

http://www.angelfire.com/journal/astrelscloset/Main_Runes.html

Another site offering online rune divinations; these are from 'Astrel's closet'.

Tarot

http://www.2.dgsys.com/~bunning/top
An online course in DIY tarot.

http://www.geocities.com/wicces_tarot/index.html
Wicce's Tarot Collection. Offers a list of tarot card decks, and reviews them for effectiveness and appearance. Also has links to other tarot sites.

http://www.osho.com
Osho-style online tarot readings à la Bhagwan shri Rajneesh.

Qabalah and alchemy

http://www.levity.com/alchemy
Alchemical Website and Virtual Library. An overwhelming 90Mbs of online information on Alchemy in all its facets, including over 200 complete alchemical texts.

http://www.qblh.org
Hermetic Alchemical Order of the QBLH. Features information about the occult and the art of the occult.

http://www.swftwtrmedia.com
Information about the mysterious Enneagram.

Numerology

http://members.aol.com/AspireA1/

A really nice site for do-it-yourself numerologists.

http://www.numberquest.com/numerology/index.html

Good source for free numerology information on the Web.

http://www.spiritlink.com/num1.html

A slightly odd site that presents a good selection of links and explanations of numerology.

http://www.askalana.com/numerology_lessons.shtml

Free lessons in numerology as presented by 'Alana'.

http://www.thedreamtime.com

A commercial website that nevertheless offers free numerology readings.

http://www.numerology.net

Download a demo version of 'professional' numerology software.

Feng Shui

Some commentators are very scathing about Feng Shui offerings on the Web, regarding much of the content as fear-based, superstitious and confusing. Here are some selections, however, from all over. You pay your money and take your pick.

http://www.fengshuinet.com
A network for Feng Shui training, information and shopping.

http://www.worldoffengshui.com
Website of the highly successful Lillian Too.

http://www.spaceclearing.com
Excellent information from Karen Kingston, the queen of clutter clearance and sacred space making.

http://www.chinesefengshui.com
Chinese Feng Shui Consultancy. An essentially commercial site that offers explanations of Feng Shui, Chinese astrology, and the biographies of several featured practitioners.

http://www.Dragonmagic.com
A geomancy site based in UK. It has been criticized for not being updated often enough.

http://www.Luckycat.com
Feng Shui goods for sale, including Tibetan and Buddhist artefacts. Based in US.

http://www.chienergy.co.uk
Website of excellent UK Feng Shui author and consultant
Simon Brown.

http://www.alt.chinese.fengshui
Feng Shui discussion and newsgroup.

http://www.fengshuisociety.org.uk
Feng Shui Society of UK.

http://www.fengshuiassociation.co.uk
Feng Shui Association of UK.

body

This section concerns itself with sites primarily covering the whole field of physical health and wellbeing. Health sites are now among the most popular areas on the Net. A recent survey rated them second only to pornography in terms of browsing popularity.

There are many excellent and large portals under the heading of holistic health and alternative medicine, which can give entry points into this approach to wellbeing as well as to many of the sub-topics listed below. As most of these will tend to be more durable than smaller sites that are more prone to coming and going, they may well be worth checking out first, so you can keep as bookmarks those that seem most suited to your own subjects of interest.

There is also a vast plethora of individual types of bodywork, physical therapy and healing, ranging from the relatively clinical and down-to-earth, to the more new-agey or even esoteric approaches.

Sex and parenting are treated in this section, so we also include the extremely well represented areas on relationships, dating and tantra, as well as stuff for kids.

14 alternative medicine

Holistic health

http://www.dmoz.org/Health/Alternative
This is part of the largest human-edited directory of the Web, and it's an open directory which means that it's not connected with one particular commercial entity. It is one of the very best sources of links on the whole field of alternative health subjects. It seems to cover the whole range of individual topics, each with their sub-categories of associated subjects, from Apitherapy (healing with bees) to Zero Balancing.

http://www.holisticmed.com
A portal that terms itself the Internet's premier resource for holistic medicine. Unfortunately the home page is very long and a bit of a pain to scroll down. But what the heck, it's worth it for the stuff you get to on this very comprehensive site.

http://www.holisticmedicine.com/fund
A guide for beginners.

http://www.tiac.net/users/mgold/health
Another good entry point, and a huge resource on holistic healing, alternative medicine and all things natural.

http://www.holisticamerica.com
A directory of holistic health sites with articles from such luminaries as Deepak Chopra.

http://www.acsh.org/dictionary
Has over 2,000 listings of terms used in alternative therapies, that can be consulted online.

http://www.earthmed.com
A very large US based site, which offers resources on everything holistic, as well as less holistic stuff such as selling vitamins. This site has inspired considerable emulation.

http://www.altguide.com
Find an alternative therapist.

http://www.channelhealth.net
A new interactive site on health in the broadest sense, linked to a digital TV health channel. Covers a wide range of health issues from a variety of experts.

http://www.naturalhealthconsultants.com
A cross-referenced database for information about health conditions and products known to be beneficial for them.

http://www.natural-healing.co.uk
A UK based directory of organizations and companies that specialize in holistic healing.

http://www.ahha.org
Promotes enhancement of health, considering the whole person: physical, emotional, mental and spiritual, as well as recognizing the part played by lifestyle choices and active participation in healing.

http://www.holisticmedicine.org

Unites western physicians who practise holistic medicine.

http://www.cyberspacehealthclinic.co.uk

A UK practitioner network and education resource, with information on over 150 health conditions and complementary health treatments. Unfortunately they insist on suggesting antibiotics for treating such conditions as athlete's foot.

http://www.achoo.com

A kind of health version of Yahoo. A fine, well organized gateway to health related resources, including a well-researched directory and hundreds of news topics to explore. Recommended.

http://www.healthy.net

The impressive home page of this attractive site offers a jumping-off point to a large number of mind-body related health topics. It does push its bookstore a bit, where you can buy over 2,000 health related publications.

http://www.mayohealth.org

An extremely impressive collection of resources; pertaining to health issues, contained in a very well designed website. A really good headline watch page will keep you up to date on the latest health issues. Not as exhaustive as **http://www.achoo.com**, but highly recommended nonetheless.

http://www.women.com
A site that focuses on women's health issues.

http://www.altmedicine.com
News pages on alternative, complementary and preventative health.

http://www.harmonyland.com/healing_net_mailing_list
Healing mailing list.

http://www.misc.health.alternatives
Newsgroup for alternatives to prescription drugs.

http://www.misc.health.alternative
Alternative health discussion newsgroup.

Complementary medicine

Complementary medicine means using the principles of holistic healing in conjunction with, or as a complement to, conventional medicine rather than as a total alternative.

http://www.ecap-online.org
This is also the official website for Bernie Siegal MD, well-loved author of such influential books as the best-selling

Love, Medicine and Miracles. The site includes details of this and other books, Bernie's teaching schedule, a specialized program for cancer patients and sufferers of other chronic illnesses using mind-body-spirit medicine, plus a discussion forum and links to other websites.

http://www.patient.co.uk
This well-organized site is edited by British doctors, and offers thousands of links to medical advice under an alphabetical health/illness directory, an online glossary of terms and a clinic search facility, as well as links to self-help and support groups, ethical healthcare and complementary treatment sites.

http://www.healthy.net/clinic/index
Complementary medicine for chronic disease.

http://www.care4free.net
A health and fitness site that covers established medical expertise as well as the full range of alternative therapies from acupuncture to yoga.

Ayurvedic medicine

http://www.dmoz.org/Health/Alternative/Ayurveda
Open Directory's 76 links on different aspects of Ayurvedic medicine from this site.

http://www.niam.com

The National Institute of Ayurvedic Medicine's site is run from its New York centre and is a good point to start from. Although it does offer the centre's services, it is also an educational resource, and as such is recommended.

http://www.ayur.com

Ayurvedic Foundation. A site dedicated to explaining the principles and benefits of ayurvedic medicine, with a good bulletin board system. An older design of website, but worth checking out.

http://www.ayurvedic.org

This is the website of the Jiva Ayurvedic Health Center. It is quite commercial in orientation, allowing you to buy ayurvedic products and literature online, but has a 'waiting room' where you can browse news articles, and a chat forum.

http://www.ayurvedahc.com

The large, if slightly ramshackle, website of another ayurvedic centre in New York. Although largely given over to the advertising of its services and correspondence courses, it is worth looking at.

http://www.veda.net

American Institute of Vedic Studies – correspondence
courses and other programs in ayurvedic medicine and
other vedic subjects.

http://www.ayur.com/message

Ayurvedic message boards.

Chinese medicine

http://www.masss.com

This Chinese medicine site comes well recommended.

Most of the sites listed under Acupuncture (see page 189)
are also relevant to this topic.

Tibetan medicine

**http://www.dmoz.org/Health/Alternative/Tibetan_
medicine**

Twenty-five links on this form of medicine, which has
some affinity with traditional Chinese medicine but has
developed in its own direction over the millennia.

Homeopathy

Note that this US spelling of the term is more commonly
used on the Net; the British spelling is Homoeopathy,
which may sometimes be useful in your choice of search
engine keywords.

http://www.dmoz.org/Health/Alternative/Homeopathy
Open Directory Project's 107 links: and in homeopathy, a little goes a long way.

http://www.homeopathyhome.com/
Homeopathy Home: a search engine, a library, an education section, chats and lots of adverts. Another good place to start.

http://www.holisticmed.com/www/homeopathy.html
A good set of links to articles and meta-directories.

http://www2.antenna.nl/homeoweb/internet.html#websites
A good collection of links to articles on the Web.

http://www.healthy.net/CLINIC/therapy/homeopat/index.asp
A good website with introductory articles and, among other things, an audio library.

http://www.hi.is/~laufeyas/
A nice website from Iceland, giving practical advice and links.

http://www.holisticmed.com/www/homeopathy
More homeopathy links.

Herbalism

http://www.dmoz.org/Health/Alternative/Herbs

Herbal links – around 277 of them!

http://www.sagemtnherbproducts.com

The simple website of a small family business specializing in herbal products, salves and tinctures. Although there is no online shop, you can buy by filling in, printing out and faxing their form.

http://www.realtime.net.anr.herbs

Reference guide for herbs.

http://www.herbnet.com

A comprehensive site for all things herbal.

http://www.planetherbs.com

A web-based discussion forum.

http://www.holisticmed.com/www/herbalism

More links on herbalism.

Flower essences

http://www.dmoz.org/Health/Alternative/Essences

Provides 35 links on flower essences from different parts of the world.

http://www.bachcentre.com

Website of perhaps the best-known proprietary branded flower essences, Mr Edward Bach's, with FAQs and publications.

http://www.spiritweb.org/Spirit/bach-flower.html

Primer on Bach flower essences.

http://www.essences.com/wwes

World Wide Essence Society. Articles and FAQs on non-Bach flower essences.

15 healing

http://www.halcyon.bizland.com
Illuminations online – 'a place to heal the body, mind and heart'.

Vibrational healing

http://www.dmoz.org/Healing/Alternative/Energy-Healing
A very fruitful 155 links to energy healing of various kinds from this excellent portal.

http://www.kirstimd.com
Journey of hearts. A substantial website collecting together writings, quotes and other resources intended to encourage those who are suffering grief and loss. A good idea founded on good intentions.

http://www.webhealing.com
Crisis, grief and healing: a portal site for many types of healing.

Reiki

http://www.dmoz.org/Health/Alternative/Reiki
You can find 216 links from this site.

http://www.reikicentrum.nl/reiki4all
A reiki webring.

http://www.masteryoftheentireuniverse.com
Level 27 mastery for you instantaneously, all free, online.
(Only joking – we made that one up.)

Crystal healing

http://www.dmoz.org/Health/Alternative/Crystals
Find 57 sparkling crystal links here.

http://www.iacht.co.uk
IACHT crystal info and sales.

Colour healing and auras

http://www.dmoz.org/Health/Alternative/Color_Therapies
31 colourful healing links.

http://www.worldlightcenter.com/litework/
An international directory of lightworkers.

http://www.themystica.com/mystica/articles/c/color_
healing.html
A good explanation of the principles of colour therapy.

http://www.mindbodyhealing.com/
A commercial site giving you the opportunity to experience colour therapy through your browser.

http://www.templeofcolour.freeserve.co.uk/index.htm
A pleasing website, with introductions to colour therapy, advertising the services of Rita Alexander in the UK.

http://www.aura.net
A popular and informative site about auras – and aura video systems.

Detoxification

http://www.holisticmed.com/www/detox
Links on all aspects of detoxification including colon therapy, saunas and fasting.

http://www.dmoz.org/Health/Alternative/Non-Toxic_Living
At the last count, 68 links.

http://www.dmoz.org/Health/Alternative/Fasting_and _Cleansing
Find 49 linked goodies, if that's your bag.

http://www.dmoz.org/Health/Alternative/Urine_Therapy
A mere 12 links for this unusual therapy.

Addiction and recovery

http://www.netaddiction.com
An online cure for addiction, rather than a cure for online addiction.

http://www.webcrafts-by-laura.com/recovery.htm
A good list of resources on recovery.

16 bodywork

http://www.bodhiwork.org
The Bodhiwork Institute: Buddhist inspired bodywork, movement and meditation.

Massage

http://www.dmoz.org/Health/Alternative/Massage
Lots of good massage links.

http://www.massageresource.com/
A good website with a searchable database of massage techniques. The place to learn about massage and bodywork.

http://www.miami.edu/touch-research/home.html
The Touch Research Institutes are dedicated to scientifically demonstrating the benefits of touch therapy.

http://www.mtwc.com
Massage Therapy Web Central.

http://members.tripod.com/~RavenwoodDals/
massage.htm
Dog massage techniques. Rub your pet.

http://www.alt.backrubs
Massage newsgroup.

Chiropractic

http://www.dmoz.org/Health/Alternative/Chiropractic
A rib-crunching 367 chiropractic links to be followed from this ever-faithful portal.

http://www.wfc.org/english/facts.html
The facts about chiropractic.

http://www.chiro.org/home.shtml
A good non-profit information site.

http://www.chiroweb.com/
Big US site, and another good place to start.

http://www.chiromed.co.uk/
Good information from this UK based site.

http://www.holisticmed.com/www/chiropractic
More links.

Osteopathy

http://www.holisticmed.com/www/osteopathy
Useful links here.

http://www.osteopathy.org.uk/
The osteopathy information page.

http://www.rscom.com/osteo/
An old site, but with good links and the 'Still Alive' electronic osteopathic journal.

http://www.americanwholehealth.com/library/osteopathy/do.htm
Good explanation of osteopathy from a nice looking site.

http://www.osteohome.com/osttext.html
A good introduction from this American site.

http://shell.break.com.au/~brettv/
An Australian site dedicated to osteopathy.

Reflexology

http://www.dmoz.org/Health/Alternative/Reflexology
Provides 82 links for you to reflect upon.

http://www.reflexology.org/index.htm
A good website with an international directory of organizations and a set of useful links.

http://www.reflexology-research.com
Summarizes scientific investigations into the effects of reflexology.

http://www.ofesite.com/health/reflex/reflexology.htm
Explanation, origins and information including charts and remedy guides.

http://medicinedreams.tripod.com/reflex.html
A simply presented page of reflexology information.

Aromatherapy

http://www.dmoz.org/Health/Alternative/Aromatherapy
Has 149 very useful and fragrant links.

http://www.naha.org
The National Association for Holistic Aromatherapy has its website here. A good collection of resources including online articles from the Aromatherapy journal.

http://www.fragrant.demon.co.uk

A simple UK based website, providing suppliers and practitioner lists for aromatherapy, as well as descriptions of oils and the symptoms they can be used to treat.

http://www.naturesgift.com

Nature's Gift aromatherapy products.

http://www.nhr.kz

Essential oils for sale, as well as aromatherapy info and news.

http://www.alt.aromatherapy

Aromatherapy discussion and newsgroup.

Biofeedback

http://www.dmoz.org/Health/Alternative/Biofeedback

Has 25 links on biofeedback.

Shiatsu

http://www.doubleclickd.com/shiatsu.html

A useful introduction to shiatsu.

http://www.shiatsu.8m.com/links.htm

A good starting point with links to many shiatsu organizations and resources.

http://www.ohashi.com/ohashiatsu.html
The commercial website of a shiatsu variation, with international directory.

http://www.healthy.net/pan/pa/bodywork/
The website of the American Oriental Bodywork Therapy Association.

http://www.imi-kiental.ch/iss.htm
A good explanation of the principles of shiatsu on this Swiss shiatsu school's website.

http://www.newcenter.edu/amma
Amma Therapy Primer on the traditional forerunner of modern clinical shiatsu.

Acupuncture and acupressure

http://www.dmoz.org/Health/Alternative/Acupuncture
A good introductory portal for acupuncture, which includes collected links for many items of interest.

http://www.acupuncture.com
A meta-directory of acupuncture and Chinese medicine resources, with links to a worldwide referral listing and schools.

http://www.acumedico.com
Articles and links on acupuncture and Chinese medicine.

http://www.americanacupuncture.com

Articles on acupuncture for smoking, weight loss, immunity, mind healing and sexual wellbeing; with lists of US medical acupuncturists.

http://www.medicalacupuncture.org

Information on acupuncture and training courses from the American Academy of Medical Acupuncture, with a search tool for practitioners in each state of the US.

http://www.medicalacupuncture.co.uk

Info from the British Medical Acupuncture Society, on medical acupuncture including access to journal articles and training courses.

http://www.acupressure.com

The Acupressure Institute.

http://www.qi-journal.com

A magazine of acupuncture and related subjects.

http://www.medicinechinese.com

FAQs and articles about acupuncture, with a consultation facility, forum and chatroom. Based in Canada.

(See also Chinese medicine, page 176.)

Magnetic therapy

http://www.dmoz.org/Health/Alternative/Magnetic_Therapy
Twenty strongly attracting links.

http://www.healthymagnets.com
Products and resources for magnetic therapy and other health purposes.

Alexander Technique

http://www.dmoz.org/Health/Alternative/Alexander
There are 70 links here on this system for wellbeing through ideal posture and movement.

http://www.alexandertechnique.com
Primer and resources on the Alexander Technique.

Yoga

http://www.dmoz.org/Religion_and_Spirituality/Yoga
There are 330 very useful links at the Open Directory's portal.

http://www.holisticmed.com/www/yoga
There are also good links to be found here.

http://www.Newageinfo.com/res/yoga

Lots of links to various schools of yoga, teaching institutes, regional information, yoga products and supplies, holidays, courses and retreats and satsangs, plus books and magazines. In among the yoga links, though, is a mass of commercially oriented links on every mind-body-spirit topic under the sun, which you may or may not find useful. Doubtful gems accessed from this site include 'how to recognize a guru' from someone who wants to lure you to his 'air-conditioned ashram with a big speaker'. Not to mention 'The River Wizard's Shop of Magic Wallpaper'.

http://www.astangayoga.co.uk

A UK based site, but this type of aerobic-oriented yoga is currently *de rigeur* in Hollywood too, among such enlightened beings as Madonna.

http://www.yogajournal.com

The website of the *Yoga Journal* includes a teacher's directory for you to find a local teacher, plus articles about yoga and its benefits to health.

http://www.siddhayoga.org

A superbly designed website, filled with information on Siddha Yoga. Worth looking at on aesthetic grounds alone, but also an excellent source of information.

http://www.piedmontyoga.com

This is a very attractive website from an Iyengar school of
yoga based in California. Worth looking at for the beauti-
ful animated GIFs of yoga movements on the first page
alone!

http://www.yoga-in-daily-life.org

Somewhat under development at the time of writing, this
website offers information on the principles of yoga and
its history, and explanations of exercises or asanas.

http://www.iyi.org.uk

Iyengar Yoga Institute. This site has links to Iyengar yoga
centres worldwide.

http://www.timages.com/yoga
Personalized yoga routines.

http://www.alt.yoga
Yoga discussion and newsgroup.

http://www.globalthink.com/yogachat
Yoga chat.

Breathwork

http://www.dmoz.org/Health/Alternative/Breathwork
Gives 25 links on breathing and breath stuff.

Martial arts

http://www.wiredaemons.com/shorinji/links.html
A good selection of martial arts links.

http://www.budoseek.net
A martial arts search engine.

http://www.taichi.com
This is the website of a Boston-based school of martial arts, specializing in tai chi and kung fu. Information on these styles, courses offered by the school, and training videos are available.

http://chineseculture.about.com/chineseculture/ msub100.htm
Good links for Chinese martial arts and wushu from the excellent 'about' portal.

http://www.aware.org
Women's self defence tutorials from this site.

http://bjj.org
A classy site dedicated to the Brazilian jiu-jitsu developed by the legendary world-beating Gracie family.

17 food

Nutrition

http://www.nutritionfocus.com

A complete source of information on food and nutrition.

http://www.cookinglight.com

A resource for healthy cooking.

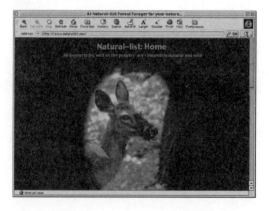

http://www.naturallist.com
Richard Nadeau is a forager for all manner of woodland and natural products, which he offers for sale from his website. Everything from fungi to deer antlers and droppings, plus a huge list of plants, are available; there are good links and photographs, too.

http://www.mynutrition.co.uk
Guidance on mixing healthy foods and vitamins.

Supplements

http://www.solgar.com
This is an excellent example of what a commercial website should be like. Simple in design and simple to understand, you can gain information on the Solgar range of nutritional supplements from here – including their shark products range – and find out where to buy them online. The site focuses on finding local suppliers for their products, but also has a large health glossary.

http://www.drweil.com
Ask Dr Weil. Advice from the well-known holistic doctor and author, including personalized supplements lists.

http://www.medmarket.com
Alternative and holistic medical products.

Vegetarianism

http://www.tiac.net/users/vrc/vrc.html

The vegetarian resource center here provides a tremendous range of links to all manner of resources related to vegetarianism.

http://www.vegweb.com

Includes features and discussion groups on vegetarianism, and thousands of recipes.

http://www.vegetariantimes.com

The Virtual Vegetarian. Magazine on vegetarian issues, and recipes too.

http://www.crazyveg.com

The crazy vegetarian website.

http://www.happycow.net

Globetrotting veggies can find listings for more than 1,600 vegetarian restaurants around the world here.

http://www.rec.food.veg

Vegetarian newsgroup.

Veganism

http://www.musonix.demon.co.uk/faq/links.htm

A nourishing mixed bag of vegan-related links.

http://www.vegansociety.com/
The fully searchable website of the Vegan Society.

http://www.globalvegetarian.com/about-veggies.htm
A tasty website including vegan and vegetarian recipes, and a good set of international links.

Allergies

http://www.allergy-info.com
A much-used and comprehensive site which often seems to be excessively slow, perhaps due in part to its popularity.

http://www.sig.net/-allergy/welcome
An allergy specialist based in Texas offers online info, plus live chat sessions.

http://www.alt.med.allergy
Allergy newsgroup.

Naturopathy

http://www.dmoz.org/Health/Alternative/Naturopathy
A useful selection of links on naturopathy.

Macrobiotics

http://www.holisticmed.com/www/macrobiotics
Useful site for macro-links. Not to be confused with macroneurotics.

18 parenting and relationships

Childbirth and pregnancy

http://www.holisticmed.com/www/birth
Links on childbirth and related subjects.

http://www.babiesonline.com/Links/Childbirth/
A good collection of sub-directories and links concerning all aspects of childbirth and related resources on the Web.

http://www.holisticmed.com/www/vaccines
For links on holistic approaches to vaccines.

Parenting

http://www.parentsoup.com
Aiming and succeeding at being a portal to almost everything you always wanted to know about being a parent. There is a daily vote on important questions such as 'Is it okay to tell a police officer that you're rushing a child

home to the bathroom to avoid a speeding ticket when your child really doesn't need to go?'

http://www.parenthoodweb.com
Clearly a major competitor to **http://www.parentsoup.com** in the parent portal stakes. Another well organized and designed site for everything from children's names to recipes.

http://www.mum2mum.com
My mum figure describes this 'a virtual cup of tea and natter with people who understand what parenting is really like'.

http://www.familyeducation.com
A site that provides information to parents on parenting.

Kids' stuff
http://www.themesh.com/feat30.html
A really nice collection of links to all manner of kids' sites. Some are Internet-based games and amusements or educational projects; others are suggestions and ideas for more traditional diversions.

http://www.kids4peace.com
A peace site for children, including stories, 'print-out-and-colour-in' drawings, a play, and more.

http://www.CreationsGuardians.com

A twelve-year-old's site, about love for nature and humanity.

http://www.funbrain.com

Online education for kids of all ages.

http://www.brainpop.com

An entertaining and interactive site for children about their brain.

http://www.waldorfworld.com

Waldorf Education matters.

http://www.netaware.org

European Union guidance on protecting children on the Net.

http://www.familyguidebook.com

American CyberAngels.

http://www.childnet-int.org

Promoting net use for children.

http://www.safekids.com

Online safety tips.

http.//www.iwf.org.uk
British Internet Watch.

alt.kids.talk
Newsgroup for kids discussing life.

(See also net filtering software on page 102.)

Sex therapy and tantra

http://www3.healthgate.com/sexualityhealth/index.asp
This is a very impressive portal site to health issues, and this page will inform you on your sexual health from a wide variety of archived articles. Interactive anatomy explorer, anyone?

http://www.askdrlove.com
Dr Love is Jamie Turndorf (gedit?), an allegedly 'internationally famous couples therapist and relationship expert who has helped millions solve their toughest love snags'. You'll find answers to hundreds of difficult love questions about 'Man who is Being Outdone by a Vibrating Machine' or 'Lady Who Agreed to a Wife Swap and Got Burned'. Entertaining and possibly illuminating.

http://www.drruth.com
The world famous sexual therapist has her site here. Apart from answering your questions, the good doctor has

provided some nice animated 'sperm mouse pointers' for your computer desktop.

http://www.intimates.com
A site with sexually and relationship-wise constructive games, which claims to be endorsed by sex therapists and marriage counsellors – as well as being fun. A free sample game is provided, but what they really want is for you to become a franchise dealer in their products.

http://www.couples-place.com
An interactive site supporting marriage and other relationships, providing information, skills training and networking opportunities. And with a name like that, I hope they don't get too many hits from would-be swingers looking for their own kind of 'networking opportunities'.

http://www.sexhealth.org/infocenter
Probably one of the most comprehensive sources of sexual health information on the Internet.

http://www.Butterflies
http://www.drwnet.com/bfly
For survivors of sexual abuse and incest, and related issues.

http://www.marsvenus.com
Venus and Mars Site of the legendary books by John Gray.

http://www.loveisgreat.com
Stuff about relationship, love and romance.

http://www.planetx.com/pooh
The Winnie the Pooh Kama Sutra. Sexual antics from the famous children's story characters, Pooh, Tigger, Eeyore and Piglet.

http://www.dmoz.org.Religion_and_Spirituality/Tantra
There are19 links here to this esoteric but increasingly popular subject.

http://www.tantra.com
If you want to get a tantric sex life, this could be for you, especially if you're duration-of-lovemakingly-challenged. It's a large commercial site that includes sacred sex related articles, forums, information on teachers and workshops. Also offers books and other products to enable you to attain 'extended full-body multiple orgasms'. With featured Position of the Month. Strong on terms like 'Female ejaculate' – is it a noun? Is it a verb? Is it a bird? There isn't much on tantric sex as a purely spiritual pursuit, though. And it doesn't mention the plumber position (you stay in all day, but nobody comes).

http://www.yOni.com

A very idiosyncratic site with a lot of appeal, particularly
if you are of the gender that has a yoni. Join for free and
enter 'the gateway to the feminine'.

*(See also Kama Sooty and Prawnography in the Humour
section, page 286.)*

Holistic dating

http://www.heavensent.co.uk

Heaven Sent dates for you.

http://www.biomatch.com

Uses biorhythm-matching methods.

http://www.naturalfriends.com

Natural Friends – a more 'holistic' dating agency, based in
the UK.

And finally ...

http://www.dmoz.org/Health/Alternative/Ear_Candling

Provides 14 links on Ear Candling (with Hopi ear candles).
It's really good.

spirit

Religion and spirituality is one of the biggest areas of interest on the Internet. It's the perfect place to put out information on every form of spiritual path from the great world religions to the tiniest sects and all kinds of other spiritual pursuits that may help us to bring meaning to our lives here on Earth. You can even see a webcam broadcast of a church service or online ordination of a priest. Let's start with some of the more general and introductory sites, which cover a number of different approaches.

The great world religions have huge web presences, covering any variations you can think of and many more besides. Then there are the other ancient spiritual paths that form an important part of the today's mind-body-spirit pantheon, such as shamanism, druidry and paganism, plus more recent developments such as neopaganism and Wicca. These last have a very great number of websites based in the US, perhaps balancing the necessarily low profile that they often have to keep there. Finally, there are a very great number of websites that come into the sometimes controversial category of cults, new religions and gurus. Just about all evangelical groups now use the Web to attract newcomers. Indeed, many of them have got into dramatic online conflict with one another, sparking violent inter-cult flame wars.

All these web presences vary in their approach to spirituality. Some are very inspirational and philanthropic in their motivation, while others are overtly commercial or even profit oriented.

We have also included in this section a variety of phenomena that have a spiritual aspect. These include mythology such as King Arthur and the Holy Grail; concern with death, past lives, out-of-body-experiences (OBEs) and altered states of consciousness. And we have also placed here sites that are to do with a 'spiritual' approach to materialism – conscious money matters, business and commerce – including the much visited 'click-charity' sites such as The Hunger Site. The increasing number of ethical investors is proof that there is a growing market for people who do not want to make money at all costs. Indeed, ethical funds are among the best performing in the market place these days. And the Internet is the ideal place to start looking for the companies and groups offering advice and products that are ethically sound – or for checking up on those that aren't.

19. religion and spirituality

http://www.religioustolerance.org

This sounds like it's just about tolerance, and it is informed by this principle, but it does much more than this. It is probably the best single resource and starting point for further searches on just about every kind of religion and spiritual path that you can think of. If you only

use one spirituality portal, this could well be your bookmark. It's a very popular site, and rightly so; about 11,000 people per week visit the home page alone.

The home page leads into pages on all the major world religions, plus ancient systems from Asatru to Voodoo and Wicca, as well as new religious movements and cults, plus other belief systems such as agnosticism, atheism and humanism. Not to mention more New Age entities such as the Osho organization and the Damanhur community. Each of these subsites includes a wonderfully clear and informative explanation of the principles and history of that belief system, followed by a list of key book references on the subject, and an assembly of relevant links to other websites.

There are a number of advertisements on the site, but it's refreshing to find that they are carefully chosen and relevant to the content, and the webmaster takes care to point out that these are what enables this non-profit site to keep going. In fact they could do with some help, so if you feel like sending a donation it will put it to very good use.

The whole site content is handled in a very sensitive and respectful manner, promoting religious diversity and covering controversial issues from all sides. This includes pages on such associated topics as equal rights, abortion, the death penalty, human cloning, suicide, slavery and genocide.

http://www.religioustolerance.org/positive.htm

This linked page gives access to a series of interesting, illuminating and inspiring articles on religious tolerance, including a chance to measure your own quota of it. There are classic statements and declarations on the subject, inspirational quotations, statements of apology for crimes against humanity, key calendar dates, and access to pages of humorous stuff. Finally, there are recommended reading lists on general aspects of religion and spirituality, and a religious tolerance webring.

http://www.dmoz.org/Society/Religion

The Open Directory. Another huge and excellent resource, consisting of over 55,000 links to sites of every religious or spiritual persuasion. Its coverage ranges from the biggies like Christianity and Buddhism to less well-known spiritual paths such as Cao Dai, Eckankar, Falun Dafa and Zoroastrianism. A branch named 'Esoteric' has 861 links of its own.

http://www.yahoo.com/society_and_culture/religion

The trusty yahoo! directory will set you off in all manner of directions if you are enquiring about religious matters.

http://www.religiousquest.com

A non-denominational and non-sectarian community of religious information and scholarship, discussion forums, history and controversy.

http://www.atlanticus.com/seeker

The seeker's guide to a range of religions and movements.

http://www.cgi.pathfinder.com/time/godcom

God.com – an online exploration of religion from *Time* magazine, featuring reporting, interviews and sound files.

http://www.religiousmovements.org

Includes many unusual faith groups.

http://www.knowledgehound.com/topics/faithspi

Spiritual and religious how-tos – such as meditating, becoming a shaman, remembering your dreams etc.

http://www.spiritualspectrum.org

RealVideo files from 14 years of TV programming on topics from meditation to capital punishment and vegetarianism to life after death.

http://www.selectsmart.com/religion

Is this cool, or what? For confused souls, anyway. Answer a few questions about your spiritual views (or lack of same) from this simple and unassuming page, for this is the URL of the belief system selector. You will be rewarded with a categorized list – in order of suitability for you – of many spiritual paths and beliefs, together with links to more information about them. Well worth a visit.

http://www.erasmus.org
An online magazine covering spiritual issues.

http://www.godserver.com
Another directory to all matters spiritual, with a vast array of links and a huge amount of information to be accessed.

http://www.soc.religion.eastern
Eastern religions newsgroup and discussion.

20 world religions

Christianity

Currently the world's leading religion, with about 33 percent of the world's population professing to practise it. This includes 87 percent of the US, with over 1,000 denominations in North America alone, from fundamentalists to liberalists.

http://religioustolerance.org/christ.htm
Comprehensive information on just about all Christian faith groups can be found at the appropriate branch of this portal, which gives an extremely good overview of Christianity and its history, and links to information on a huge variety of individual denominations from Amish to the Way. It also has sub-pages on such controversial topics as virgin birth, resurrection, hell, the shroud of Turin and the importance of being 'saved'. Discussion includes comments from many different points of view; for instance you can even click to see 'quite angry and

hateful' comments, which have their very own link. It's good to know you're being heard.

http://www.christianityonline.com
A Christian search engine.

http://www.home.vistapnt.com/markm
Christian naturists. Anyone who does not worship God in the nude would probably describe Pastor Mark and his Christian naturists as eccentric. As seems to be the naturist way, they are keen to show you pictures.

http://www.jesusmysteries.demon.co.uk
The site for the best-selling book *The Jesus Mysteries*, which suggests that the historical Jesus figure may have been the recurrence of an identical pre-Christian archetypal deity.

http://www.greenspirit.com
Site of creation-centred spirituality, celebrating all of existence as profoundly interconnected and inherently sacred.

http://www.jesus.org.uk
The British Jesus Army.

http://www.alt.religion.christian
Christian newsgroup and discussion.

Buddhism

For whatever reason, Buddhist websites as a whole have a reputation for being groovier and more coolly designed than most of your average religious websites. In terms of entry points, as well as Religious Tolerance's Buddhism branch there's the Open Directory's portal: **http://www.dmoz.org/society/Religion_and_Spirituality/Buddhism**. It's a lot to key in, but it will give you a thumping 2,098 variously Buddhistic links!

http://www.buddhanet.net
Buddhist Information Network. This is a very beautifully presented portal site that includes Buddhist web links and the BuddhaNet search engine.

http://www.dharmanet.org

Dharma Net International. One of the first and largest Buddhist sites on the Web, run online by one person since 1991 as an offering to the world. It thinks of itself as 'a cross-roads for international Buddhism'.

Types of Buddhism

http://www.sgi.org

SGI International's website for Nichiren Buddhism, a form of Buddhism which originated in Japan but is increasingly followed in the West today, based on chanting Nam-Myoho-Renge-Kyo.

http://www.quietmountain.com

International resources and teachings relating to Tibetan Buddhism and Tibet. An excellent and good-looking site for this subject, with lots of information and links. It contains articles on the different main schools of Tibetan Buddhism: Nyingmapa, Sakyapa, Kagyupa and Gelugpa, as well as on the art and culture of Tibet. It also has Buddhist chat and a chance to buy artefacts online – presumably without attachment. And free Dharma screensavers. And RealAudio prayers.

http://www.Zenguide.com

Despite its name, this site has material on most Buddhist traditions as well as Zen. It's a nicely designed and presented site which explains the basic concepts of Buddhism and its history. It provides information on Buddhist temples and organizations in the US and around the world, and provides an online discussion group. You may even find out what Zen has to do with archery, business or motorcycle maintenance.

http://www.members.aol.com/zenunbound
A Zen Buddhism resource.

http://www.alt.buddha.short.fat.guy
http://www.alt.zen
Buddhist newsgroups and discussion.

http://www.edepot.com/buddha
Buddhist chat.

Islam

http://www.dmoz.org/society/Religion_and_
Spirituality/Islam
A good entry point – the Open Directory's portal where there are over a thousand links on all aspects of Islam.

http://www.latif.com
A selection of Islamic links.

http://www.musalman.com
An Islam search engine.

http://www.sunnah.org
'One of the top Islamic sites in the world'. Turn your speakers up for the introductory audio to this huge website.

http://www.islamicity.org
Live radio broadcasts including prayer, plus text material about Islam and its history.

http://www.ummah.org.uk
Islamic Gateway. UK-based, magazine-style site with offerings on Islam, including Koran extracts in multimedia format.

http://www.alt.religion.islam
http:\\www.soc.religion.islam
Islamic newsgroups and discussion.

Sufism

http://www.sufism.org/society/index.html#sufism
Representing the Mevlevi order of Jalaladin Rumi with some extensive articles and links.

http://www.krela.com/about/sufism.shtml
A really fine personal page discussing some of the ideas of Sufism.

http://inspirationalstories.com/2_sfm.html
A collection of Sufi stories from this interesting story-telling site.

Hinduism

http://www.dmoz.org/society/Religion_and_Spirituality/Hinduism
Here you will find a worthwhile 420 links on Hinduism.

http://www.hindunet.org
Hindu philosophy, teachings, culture and customs.

http://www.hindu.org
Hindu Resources Online.

http://www.alt.hindu
Moderated Hindu newsgroup.

Hare Krishna

http://www.islandnet.com/krsna
This is a confusingly designed site for anyone who is not a Krishna devotee, and even they may have difficulty finding their way around here. Has a large list of articles, though.

Judaism

http://www.dmoz.org/society/Religion_and_
Spirituality/Judaism
Provides 1,255 links.

http://www.jewish.com/search
A Judaic search engine.

http://www.jewishlinks.net
A Jewish and Israeli directory with thousands of community directories and links worldwide.

http://www.maven.co.il
Jewish and Israeli links.

http://www.generationj.com
Cool information for young-ish Jews.

http://www.soc.culture.jewish
Jewish newsgroup and discussion.

Taoism

The ancient Chinese religion of Lao Tsu (or Tse), revitalized in the West by Alan Watts et al. It's pronounced 'dow', and is the origin of Tai Chi and other systems. 'Be still like a mountain and flow like a great river' ... Sounds like a great affirmation to adopt as you surf the Net.

http://www.religioustolerance.org/taoism.htm

Information on the history, beliefs, practices and texts of Taoism, such as the Tao te Ching; plus inspirational quotations such as the above. And of course web links too.

**http://www.dmoz.org/society/Religion_and_
Spirituality/Taoism**

Useful Taoist links.

http://www.taoresource.com

Here's just what you've been looking for. Taoist products and artefacts, such as you will need 'to build a small Taoist shrine or even to construct a large Taoist temple' – effortlessly, no doubt.

Sikhism

http://www.sikhseek.com

A Sikh search engine

Baha'i

**http://www.dmoz.org/society/Religion_and_
Spirituality/Baha'i**

Provides 217 links on Baha'i.

Zoroastrianism

**http://www.dmoz.org/society/Religion_and_
Spirituality/Zoroastrianism**

Has 39 links on Zoroastrianism.

Rastafarianism

**http://www.dmoz.org/society/Religion_and_
Spirituality/Rastafarianism**

Gives 30 links on Rastafarianism.

African Religion

http://www.users.iol.it/cdi

Useful starting point for African traditional religions.

21 ancient spirituality

Shamanism

**http://www.dmoz.org/society/Religion_and_
Spirituality/Shamanism**

There are 81 shamanistic links from this site.

http://www.cybershaman.co.uk/html/shamanism.html

An unpretentious site that attempts to explain shamanism and show the worldwide variations and similarities that occur.

http://deoxy.org/shaman.htm

A nice website with realaudio files, and links mainly concerning South American Ayahuasca shamanism.

http://anamspirit.com/shamanism.html

Shamanism in Ireland presented by Joe Mullally.

http://www.hist.unt.edu/09w-ar7l.htm

A list of links related to shamanism and Carlos Castaneda.

http://www.dmoz.org/society/Religion_and_
Spirituality/Huna

Provides 39 links on Huna, the Hawaiian form of shamanistic spirituality.

http://www.shamanism.co.uk

Eagle's Wing – a British based site with useful links for
shamanism. Check out the excellent 'words of inspiration'.

Celts and druidry

Modern druidism is one of the neopagan family of belief
systems that recreate ancient practices for modern times.
The Celtic culture to which they belonged continues to be
an ever more popular source of inspiration and wisdom.

http://www.dmoz.org/society/Religion_and_
Spirituality/druid

The Open Directory provides yet another excellent introduction to this subject. This portal provides informative
descriptions of the history, mythology, deities, beliefs and
practices, modern orders of druidry and books, as well as
correcting popular misconceptions such as the practice of
ritual killing. There is direct access to information on
topics such as the use of ancient monuments, for

example Stonehenge and Avebury, and information on key figures like Cerridwen, Arawn and Lugh, and the great Celtic feasts or days of celebration.

http://www.celt.net
A fantastic resource including a free web hosting service, archives, and links including the searchable encyclopaedia of the Celts. Recommended.

http://www.sunsite.unc.edu/gaelic/celts
This site offers an overview of Celtic culture.

http://www.celtic.net/
Celtic online community with good links and resources.

http://www.celts.org/
A simple design and a good website from Ireland with genealogical links.

http://www.optimizations.com/Celts/links.html
A good selection of links on Celtic stuff.

Druidic organizations
http://www.druidry.org
Order of Bards, Ovates and Druids.

http://www.druidorder.demon.co.uk
British Druid Order.

http://www.keltria.org
The Henge of Keltria.

http://www.adf.org
Ar nDraiocht Fein.

http://www.alt.religion.druid
Druidry newsgroup and discussion.

Paganism

Paganism is essentially the collection of spiritual practices that existed in Europe before the Romans introduced Christianity. It's an incredibly well-followed spiritual path, especially in the US, but is not always out in the open because of prejudice and misunderstanding.

http://www.dmoz.org/society/Religion_and_ Spirituality/Pagan
There are 1,942 links on Paganism here – more than the corresponding portals for Judaism, Hinduism or Islam. There's a vast amount of stuff about it on the Web.

http://www.search.paganforest.com
A 'Yahoo-like' search engine.

http://www.omphalos.net

Describes itself as 'the centre of the pagan web' and would appear to be so. An excellently designed portal/directory.

http://www.newavalon.com

An e-zine 'for the modern pagan' with a searchable index and a good range of discussion topics in its forum.

http://www.alt.pagan

Pagan newsgroup and discussion.

Norse Paganism

This is now often known as Asatru, a modern revival of the ancient northern pagan religion from Norse, Icelandic, German and Anglo-Saxon sources. It's full of wonderful ancient words such as heathen, wyrd, frithstead, harrow and futhark, as well as cool gods like Odin, Woden and Thor.

http://www.newageinfo.com.res.asatru

Lots of links covering information on individual areas and branches of the tradition, as well as ancient sacred places, runes, herbology, festivals and chat groups for Nordic gossip.

http://www.religioustolerance.org/asatru.htm

The Religious Tolerance site on Norse Paganism.

(See also Runes, page 162.)

Neopaganism

Neopaganism is the name generally given to relatively modern revivals of the ancient pagan pre-Christian European religions, although different people tend to use the word differently, and some of these don't sound like very spiritual people at all.

http://www.neopagan.net

The improbably named Isaac Bonewits has created a website of very simple design, concerning his interests of paganism, witchcraft and druidism. Idiosyncratic, but no worse for that.

http://branwenscauldron.com

Sells supplies for Neopagans and Wiccans.

Wicca and witchcraft

Wicca is a recently created neopagan religion, based on indigenous European spirituality. It has little to do with the Harry Potter version of witchcraft and magic, or the fairy-tale idea of horrid little women with terrible dress sense, casting evil spells and eating children in their hovels in the woods.

http://www.religioustolerance.org/witchcra.htm

As usual, this site gives an excellent overview of its subject, correcting many wrong impressions and misinformation about Wicca that stem from medieval hysteria. It also clarifies terms such as witchcraft and paganism. There are direct links to on-site pages on its history and development, beliefs and practices and symbols, with lots of particulars such as pentagrams, pentacles and handfasting ceremonies. There's also much material on the 'burning times' and on media coverage and bias. And there are lists of books and links to other sites.

http://www.witchvox.com
A truly extraordinary website dedicated to Wicca and witchcraft. Without doubt the definitive site on the Net on this subject – an enormous creation.

http://www.wiccanet.com
A multi-function site featuring news, resources and information, with hundreds of links to websites, webrings and suppliers of products and services.

http://www.circlesanctuary.org
Provides worldwide networking for Wiccans and other Pagans of many paths and traditions.

http://www.witchesweb.com
A large Wiccan site.

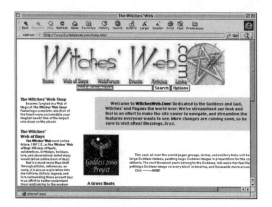

http://www.wiccan-refuge.com

Describes the basis of Wiccan beliefs and practices, plus
books and so on.

Mythology

http://www.dmoz.org/Arts/Literature/Myths

Links on mythology, some with a literary slant.

http://www.dreamtime.net.au

Stories of the Dreaming – Australian aboriginal creation
stories in a variety of media formats, with pictures and
sound.

http://www.religioustolerance.org/druid.htm

Links on Celtic mythology.

http://www.newageinfo.com/res/asatru

Contains information and links on Norse mythology.

http://www.windows.umich.edu/cgi-bin/tour_def/ mythology/mythology.html

An attractive site from the University of Michigan. Use these pages to find out about the gods and goddesses of different cultures around the world, and the works of art people have created to give them expression. A nice links section includes 'myth of the month'.

http://www.pitt.edu/~dash/folktexts.html

A comprehensive archive of folklore and mythology electronic texts collated by the University of Pittsburgh.

http://www.digital-librarian.com/mythology.html

A fine collection of links from the excellent Digital Librarian covering all aspects of mythology.

http://www.pantheon.org/mythica/

The Encyclopedia Mythica contains over 5,100 definitions of gods and goddesses, supernatural beings, and legendary creatures and monsters from all over the world.

http://www.mythinglinks.org/jungian~etc.html
A well-researched collection of links including Jungian and dream research resources, and links to foundations, institutes and associations working in the field.

(See also Indigenous Peoples, page 270.)

Holy Grail, Arthurian legends and Merlin

http://www.yi.com/home/AntonioMendonca/templars
A site about the Knights Templar, the alleged guardians of the Holy Grail.

http://dc.smu.edu/Arthuriana/
The home page of the journal of Arthurian studies including a links section to a selection of Arthurian resources on the Web.

http://www.angelfire.com/me2/camelot/
A simple and attractive website developed from a student project by 'the Lady of Shalott'. Images, links and an A-Z of the legends and the characters of the Arthurian myth.

http://www.georgetown.edu/labyrinth/
A fully searchable database of resources on medieval culture, including a special section of Arthurian studies material. Truly labyrinthine in scope.

http://www.mystical-www.co.uk/merlin/

An informative page on Merlin from an extensive portal site on all matters mystical.

Mysticism

http://www.dmoz.org/society/Religion_and_Spirituality/ mysticism

Provides 225 links on mysticism in its different aspects.

http://www.themystic.org

Mysticism from beginner to advanced level.

http://www.spiritnetwork.com

Spirituality, wellness and the paranormal.

22 other spiritual phenomena

New religions and cults

A lot of new religious movements (or NRMs) are moving their chief activity arena to the Internet, using it to attract newcomers. The term 'cult' is often used to describe many of these groups, usually in a derogatory sense. Likewise there has grown up a whole industry of anti-cult activities, which have an equally high web profile. Antagonism between these various groups often results in online flame wars. Here is a selection of web presences in these different areas.

http://www.religioustolerance.org/cultmenu.htm
Ironically, this is an excellent introduction to the subject of cults and NRMs, most of which we are assured are 'quite harmless'; on the other hand, they also supply information on destructive and 'doomsday' cults at **http://www.religioustolerance.org/destruct.**

http://www.guardian.co.uk/observer/cults
An A-Z of Cults, based in UK.

http://www.levelabovehuman.org
Website of the Heaven's Gate group.

http://www.subgenius.com
Church of the Subgenius – visit here to meet the man with the pipe, and find out about the worship of 'slack'.

http://www.xenu.net
Home of Operation Clambake and the Cult Information Centre, a charity that offers support and advice about cults and their tactics.

http://www.ex-cult.org
Life after cults.

http://www.rickross.com
Website of exit counsellor Rick Ross, who rescues people from cults.

http://www.talk.religion.newage
Discussion on New Age religions.

Gurus and teachers

http://www.kheper.auz.com/topics/gurus/gurus.html
An interesting website, basic in design but insightful of content. Includes a small tabulated list of gurus and teachers, informed comment, and the current status of each.

http://www.lanset.com/spiritinfo/pages/crucible2.html
Guru questions – an excellent template of questions based on criteria suggested by both Eastern and Western spiritual traditions, that can help seekers judge contemporary teachers, gurus and movements.

http://www.wideopenwin.com/dynamic.html
An enormous database website which intends to offer, as a creative expression of present-time enlightenment, the most complete listing of self-realized teachers who have a presence on the World Wide Web today. An extensive selection of links.

http://www.pscw.uva.nl/sociosite/TOPICS/religion.html
Not just an index to gurus and teachers, but a comprehensive resource from which to research spiritual paths.

http://www.hindulinks.org/God_Sages_and_Gurus/
A good collection of links covering Hindu gurus and sages, ancient and modern.

http://www.anthroposophy.net
Rudolf Steiner and his works.

http://www.elib.com/Steiner
The Rudolf Steiner Archive – everything to do with Anthroposophy – books, lectures, pictures and links.

http://www.osho.com
Online tarot, daily meditations and e-commerce from the artist formerly known as Bhagwan Shri Rajneesh. There is also a site at **http://www.osho.org**

Consciousness

http://www.newdimensions.org
New Dimensions Radio: explores social, environmental and spiritual frontiers through radio and TV interviews with many of today's foremost social innovators, thinkers, scientists and creative artists.

http://www.globalcommunity.org
The Foundation for Global Community has been going for half a century, so it must be doing something right.

http://www.interspecies.com
Interspecies Communication – get brain endorphin release from online dolphin sonics (that means 'squeaks').

http://www.healthjourneys.com
Books, tapes and resources on guided imagery.

http://www.alt.consciousness
Conscious discussion and newsgroup.

Channelling

http://www.spiritweb.org/Spirit/channellings
A gallery of channellers with their pictures, biographical info, channelled writings, articles, guidance and accounts of how they came to be doing what they're doing. For example, Daryl Anka who began channelling an extraterrestrial called Bashar after experiencing two UFO sightings and then remembered having made a past life agreement to perform the service of channelling this entity. Daryl and Bashar now together provide cutting-edge information on the nature of the universe and 'how to create the reality that you desire'.

http://www.tsl.org
The Ascended Master Network – 325 miscellaneous linked channelling websites assorted by flavour e.g. ascension related channelling, metaphysical channelling, animal related channelling, nature related channelling, native prophecies, poetry channellings and channelling chat.

http://www.ramtha.com

Ramtha's School of Enlightenment: teachings of the American Agnostic school, based on the channellings from Ramtha by J. Z. Knight.

http://www.iamamerica.com

Lori Toye claims to be a prophet of 'earth changes' transmitted to her from higher beings; her interpretations of their transmissions largely comprise illustrated maps which you can buy online. Judge for yourself.

http://www.michaelteachings.com

The Michael soul group is a collective entity of souls, which channels its teachings through this website's creator (among others). You can find out more from here, including testimonials to the teaching's power and its connections to extra terrestrial life.

http://www.alt.paranormal.channeling

Channelling newsgroup and discussion.

Out of Body Experiences (OBEs) and astral travel

Also known as astral projection or interdimensional travelling, OBEs (not Order of the British Empire) are all the rage these days, and are well represented on the Net. Here are a few examples to set you on your journey.

http://www.spiritweb.org/spirit/obe

Provides OBE and astral projection related definitions, explanations and guides. There are also OBE FAQs and chat. For instance, if I am projecting astrally, can I meet or talk to people? And when I have an OBE, can I see in the dark? There are also lots of first person accounts of experiences, how to have them and what to expect. There are helpful diagrammatic pictures of the astral body leaving the physical body. Hospital seems to be a popular location – especially in conjunction with a Near Death Experience (NDE). People on this site seem to be out of their bodies a great deal. One wonders whether there is such a thing as a OME (Out of your Mind Experience)?

http://www.lava.net/~goodin/astral

The astral projection home page. The words 'home page' take on a whole new meaning in this context.

http://www.eckankar.org

Soul-travelling, light and the sound of God.

http://www.alt.out-of-body

OBE discussion and newsgroup.

Atlantis

http://www.atlan.org

A well laid out, informative website. Recommended.

http://www.truorigins.net/atlantis
The legend explained in quasi-religious terms, including the Atlantean names given by Edgar Cayce.

http://www.mysteries-megasite.com/atlantis/atlantis-2.html
Source of 500 links on Altantis.

Angels

http://www.angelhaven.com/
For all things Angelic.

http://www.lutz-sanfilippo.com/library/lsfangels.html
A doctoral essay on angels as spiritual guides.

http://www.riverblast.com/songofazrael/
A website dedicated to the guardian angel of souls.

http://www.angels4peace.com
A collection of poems, features and art about angels and how they will lead the way to peace on earth.

http://members.aol.com/Angelcomix/index.html
A comic strip about an angel named Steve.

Dolphins

http://fp.premier1.net/iamdavid/healing.html
Dolphin facilitated healing articles. Nice site.

http://www.lemurianvisions.com
Linking Atlantis to dolphins, in religious terms.

http://www.sto-p.com/dp/dolfaq.htm
An interesting set of dolphin FAQs.

http://website.lineone.net/~webjungle/
Site of the Alexander Trust, set up to assist a young boy's dolphin therapy.

23 spiritual events

http://www.festival.com
A huge list of festivals and celebrations.

http://www.welcomehome.org
Info, news and Rainbow Gatherings events.

http://www.worldpeaceday.com
A worldwide day of prayer for global healing, each summer solstice.

http://www.hyperlinker.com/earthcal
The Earth's calendar.

http://www.thirdmill.com
The Third Millennium Calendar of events metaphysical, holistic and spiritual.

http://www.religioustolerance.org/summer_solstice.htm
http://www.religioustolerance.org/winter_solstice.htm
http://www.religioustolerance.org/druid.htm
Solstice- and Equinox-related resources.

24 death and the spirit

Deathwork

http://www.mydeath.net

This is a place for people to register what they want done, said, played or read at their funeral, and whether they want to be buried or burnt, on land or at sea, what the mourners should wear, and anything at all that you want to specify. Plus you can see what other people have said they want. Great idea.

http://www.whatawaytogo.com

Slightly different ways to say goodbye, such as scattering ashes from a hot air balloon, or launching them into space in a rocket. Seriously.

http://www.goodgriefgroups.com

A support program for organizations that help the bereaved.

http://www.kirstimd.com
Journey of hearts. A website that collects together writings, quotes and other resources intended to encourage those who are suffering grief and loss.

http://www.webhealing.com
Crisis, grief and healing – a portal site for different forms of healing.

http://www.adec.org
Association for Death Education and Counselling,

http://www.lightning-strike.com
Lightning Strike Pet-Loss Support Page. The ultimate resource for all recently bereaved pet owners. Messages can be left by or sent to the bereaved.

Past lives and reincarnation

http://www.dmoz.org/society/Religion_and_Spirituality/Reincarnation
Provides 55 links that reach beyond the present life.

http://www.reincarnation-org.com
Reincarnation-related web resources.

http://www.after-death.com/links/lad
Life after death – links to a wide variety of websites that offer differing perspectives on life beyond physical death.

http://www.worble.com/LifeAfterDeath
Religious perspectives on life after death – links to views on the concept from the world's main religions.

Near Death Experiences (NDEs)

These involve dying and then changing your mind, and coming back to deal with unfinished business. Like Out of Body Experiences (OBEs), NDEs are also becoming more of a commonplace experience. Everyone deserves one these days, it seems.

http://www.dmoz.org/Society/Death/Near_Death_Experiences
Gives 73 links on NDEs.

http://www.near-death.com
More NDE resources.

http://www.spiritweb.org/Spirit/nde.html
Another good portal for NDEs.

http://www.near-death.com/cayce
Edgar Cayce and NDEs.

25 spiritual finance

Business and trade

http://www.enviroweb.org/issues/enough

The Never Enough campaign connects the problems of world poverty, environmental destruction and social alienation to the consumerist lifestyle. The campaign advocates different ways of living, trading and working in order to 'live more lightly' on the Earth, and calls for a fairer distribution of resoures. A fine site with spoof advertisements and sensible critique.

http://www.newagebiz.com

An online resource for New Age or mind-body-spirit business people, retail store owners, wholesalers, distributors or manufacturers, supporting business development both on- and off-line.

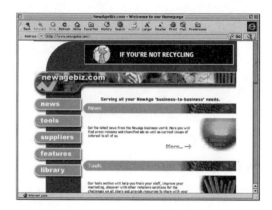

http://www.sustainablebusiness.com

The place to come to gain hard information on sustainable business. A serious website with sections for those who wish to set up environmentally responsible concerns, news and features.

http://www.envirolink.org/sbn

Sustainable Business Network – information and connections for working towards a green economy.

http://www.prosperity.com

Prosperity and abundance – a spiritually oriented site, which includes use of the Enneagram.

http://www.dropthedebt.org

Movement to cancel crippling third world debts, instigated by Bono of U2 and supported by Mohamed Ali, the Pope and many other luminaries.

http://www.equalexchange.com

Provides a list of organizations promoting global fair trade.

http://www.amorenaturalway.com

New Age management – a website for enlightened managers, bringing in principles from the natural world.

http://www.coopamerica.org

Co-op America: an alliance of nearly 2,000 socially responsible businesses with nearly 50,000 members in the US. They also run National Green Pages Online at **http://www.coopamerica.org/gp/**

Ethical investment

http://www.greenmoney.com

Gain information on how to spend and invest your money ethically. A huge collection of international resources, as well as articles and news on environmental issues. Lists of socially responsible banks and credit unions. 'Responsibility, from the Supermarket to the Stockmarket.'

http://www.goodmoney.com
Company profiles, news and 'how to' guides.

http://www.calvertgroup.com
Socially responsible investing.

http://www.ethicalinvestors.co.uk
As the above tend to be US-biased, this alternative is worth visiting for UK investors, particularly in the light of the new possibilities opened up by recent government regulations.

http://www.ethicalservices.co.uk
Ethical Investment Services – jargon-free breakdown of the type of investments available, plus information and news on the growing ethical investment sector. Includes an interactive ethical fund selector. You have to register, but they do carry out ethical screening of companies and products.

Charity donation sites

When you click on these sites, a donation is made by the sponsors to the charity concerned. You can visit them up to once a day.

http://www.thehungersite.com
The much-visited Hunger Site.

http://www.rainforest.care2.com
Race for the Rainforest.

http://www.saverainforest.net
Save the Rainforest site.

earth

Environment and community related websites form a very important and influential part of Internet content these days. In the arena of green campaigning, for instance, Internet communication has opened up new possibilities for influencing public opinion and awareness, spreading news quickly and making direct action more effective. In Northern Tasmania, a tree lover named Hector the Protector kept loggers at bay for twelve days as he sat high up in a threatened gum tree. His reports of the devastation of the landscape were sent to the world via his website at **http://www.nfu.org.au/up-a-tree**, updated day by day by mobile phone. That website attracted a lot of publicity, and is still campaigning even though the tree is now sadly gone. Green-unfriendly aspects of McDonalds' global business have been highlighted on the world stage by the operators of the McSpotlight website at **http://www.mcspotlight.org**.

Since we are also dealing here with communities, this section goes on to deal with ethnic groups and then with those somewhat specialized communities, 'women' and 'men'.

26 environment and ecology

http://www.greenpeace.org
An absolutely superb website – the paradigm against which all activist and awareness websites must be judged – international in vision and implementation, excellent in design and navigation, informative in content.

http://www.foe.org
Friends of the Earth – the highly influential organization dedicated to preservation and protection of the Earth's resources, which operates both at grassroots level and in influencing national governments and the UN.

http://www.oneworld.org/earthaction
Earth action movement. An impressive information resource intended to educate all on key environmental and social issues, with a remarkable campaign archive and advice for those wishing to take direct action.

http://iisd1.iisd.ca

The Canadian International Institute for Sustainable Development seeks to develop policies for the international political community to advance its agenda for sustainable growth. A serious website for serious concerns.

http://www.worldwatch.org

The Worldwatch Institute is dedicated to fostering the evolution of an environmentally sustainable society; its website is extensive and includes its magazine, archives, an audio stream, and an up-to-date set of 'Issue Alerts' from the media.

http://www.millenniuminstitute.net

The Millennium Institute is a commercial organization dedicated to providing tools, policies and analyses of environmental awareness to policy makers worldwide. Chief among these is a computerized system, the Threshold 21 (T21) Integrated Development Model.

http://www.ucsusa.org

This fascinating and well-designed website is the online presence of the Union of Concerned Scientists. It is clearly and simply presented, offering not only information but also strategies to make a difference.

http://www.envirolink.org
Ostensibly the largest online environmental service on this particular planet.

http://www.enn.com
Environmental Newsletter – latest news on environmental issues.

http://www.ethical-junction.org
This site has been launched to guide surfers through the increasingly congested area of eco-cyberspace.

http://www.life.ca
Natural Life Online Directory – a green Canadian portal website.

http://www.greenmap.org
Green Map System – US regional green info.

http://www.gn.apc.org
Green Net. This is a 'green' London-based ISP, which boasts a large number of ethically aware clients for whom it provides a fully featured suite of hosting services.

http://www.ecomall.com
Something like a virtual town of ecological shops.

Nature awareness and conservation

http://www.ecopsych.com

This interesting site is about Project Nature Connect from the Institute of Global Education, a consultant NGO body to the UN Economic and Social Council. It's a good-looking, well-organized, quick-loading site that is concerned with education and counselling methods that are inspired by connection with the natural world.

http://www.purpleturtle.com

This site is about the fortunes of a pair of turtles named Purple and Destiny. A free email provider donates 20 percent of its banner advertising revenues to the Caribbean Conservation Fund, which runs turtle sponsorship programs like this among its other activities.

http://www.panda.org

World Wide Fund for Nature.

http://www.charityfrogs.org

Visit this website and its sponsors will donate money 'for your click' to the American Red Cross.

http://www.saverainforest.net

Clicking here (you're only allowed to do so once a day) will give money (from sponsors) to save the rainforest.

http://www.rainforest.care2.com

A similar way to make a donation to save the rainforest – these websites are an excellent idea, and well worth clicking on to.

Sustainable development

http://www.greensense.com

A huge resource on sustainable living from Green Sense.

http://www.rmi.org

The Rocky Mountain Institute – the influential foundation for non-profit research and education, supporting individuals, organizations and the private sector. It focuses on finding 'new solutions to old problems' by 'harmonizing the power of market economics and advanced techniques for resource efficiency'.

http://www.awaken.com
Awakening Technology. These people 'grow knowledge' for use in cyberspace, at the intersection of business, information technology, community and spirit.

http://www.un.org/esa/sustdev
This is the address of the United Nations Commission on Sustainable Development. Like much of the UN website, well designed and informative.

http://www.cat.org.uk
The Centre for Alternative Technology is based in Wales. This is an attractive, if small-scale, website from 'Europe's foremost eco-centre', and includes information on the international environmental Agenda 21.

http://www.sustainable.doe.gov
The American Government's website on sustainable development is extensive and has a wide selection of resources including its 'topics on sustainability'.

http://www.cnt.org/
The Center for Neighborhood Technology aims to promote environmentally friendly and sustainable initiatives at grassroots level. Based in Chicago, its ideas are spreading and its attractive website is well worth looking at.

http://www.cool-companies.org
Website of the Centre for Energy and Climate Solutions.

http://www.gaia.org
The Global Ecovillage Network. A non-profit, grassroots organization, which links together eco-villages with related projects around the world. This well-presented and visually interesting site has admirable aims and features.

Organic growing

http://www.organickitchen.com/gardening.html
A guide to organic food and gardening information available on the Web.

http://library.envirolink.org/
A comprehensive and searchable resource of environmental information with a large plant database.

http://www.purefood.org
Website of the Organic Consumers Association.

http://www.netspeed.com.au/cogs/cogdef.htm
A set of definitions as to what organic growing actually means, from the Canberra Organic Growers' Society.

http://www.rain.org/~sals/my.html

The huge, long home page of an organic grower. Humorous and thought-provoking.

http://thegardenhelper.com

Organic gardening tips, advice, and articles by organic farmer and author Mort Mather.

Permaculture

http://www.sonic.net/~lberlin/hotspots.html

A fertile set of links for permaculturists.

http://www.permacult.com.au/research.html

A useful set of topics concerning organic growing, permaculture and ecology.

http://www.earthaven.org/

The website of an ecovillage community, developing permaculture on 325 acres in the Southern Appalachian Mountains of North Carolina, USA.

Genetic modification

http://www.greenpeace.org/~geneng/

Learn how to avoid GM foods, and how to protest about them.

http://www.geneticfoodalert.org.uk

Genetic Food Alert.

http://www.gn.apc.org/pmhp/gs
Genetics Snowball.

http://www.vibrantplanet.com/geneticconcern
Genetics Concern.

http://www.geneticsanction.org.uk
The Genetic Engineering Network.

http://www.ucs.org
The Union of Concerned Scientists.

http://www.psrast.org
Physicians and Scientists for Responsible Application of Science and Technology.

http://www.south-asianinitiative.org/wff
Website of Karnataka State Farmers Association, India.

http://www.gmworld.newscientist.com
Scientific coverage of the GM foods debate from this respectable UK based magazine.

http://www.geneticsforum.co.uk
Website of the Genetics Forum.

http://www.foodbiotech.org/
Take a look here at the opposite side of the argument.

Earth mysteries
http://www.sacredsites.com/
An excellent website compiled by anthropologist and photographer Martin Gray. Martin has visited and photographed over 1,000 sacred sites in 70 countries. Recommended.

http://www.indigogroup.co.uk/edge/
An archive of articles originally published in *At the Edge* magazine and its predecessor, *Mercian Mysteries*. *At the Edge* aimed to 'walk on the cracks' between archaeology, mythology and folklore.

http://www.activemind.com/Mysterious/Topics/Stonehenge
The ActiveMind site on Stonehenge.

http://www.danwinter.com/sitemap.html
'The animations and images of the mind-twisting science and physics of consciousness, based on the sacred geometry of the heart.'

http://www.starwheels.com/
The highly attractive mandala pages of the artist Aya.

Ley lines and crop circles

http://www.leyhunter.com/

Website of the Leyhunter journal, with an emphasis on archaeostronomy and British megalithic sites.

http://www.wire.net.au/~melinda/ley.htm

A good set of research resources into ley lines, including 'research topics to make you wonder'.

http://www.circlemakers.com

Crop circles. This is an extraordinary website and is unequivocally recommended. The photographs of crop circles are truly remarkable, and the design, if a little dark, fits its subject matter.

http://www.paradigmshift.com
Crop circle central – all the theories on their creation, from ley lines to plasma vortices.

27 community

http://www.ic.org
The Intentional Communities' website is of simple design
and comprehensive scope. It includes a resources section,
cross-reference charts, recommended reading list, photos
and indexes.

http://fic.ic.org
The Fellowship for Intentional Community. Information on 500 intentional communities (rather than
accidental ones) plus 250 alternative resources and
services.

http://www.findhorn.org
Website of the pioneering and highly influential Scottish
New Age Findhorn Community.

http://www.globalvisions.org/cl/spiritmesa
The Spirit Mesa Project is a proposed global village for

cultural arts and media for a better world. It's a good looking site with description of the project, a mission statement, progress report, FAQs and how to participate, support or invest in it.

http://www.welcomehome.org
A loosely knit hippie tribe, which holds occasional Rainbow Gatherings that are 'entirely non-commercial and very counter-cultural'.

http://www.hippy.com
Hippyland. Self-explanatory, probably. 'A colourful fun website', they say.

Indigenous peoples

http://www.nativeweb.org
A website for the Earth's indigenous peoples.

http://www.thegarden.net/uwa
The U'wa Information Center – supports the native U'wa people of Colombia, who are threatened with the destruction of their homeland by oil companies.

http://www.quietmountain.com
Quiet Mountain Tibetan Resource Guide. Articles on Tibet, Bhutan, Ladakh or Little Tibet, the Free Tibet movement, traditional medicine and music, and with maps and

images of Tibet. There is also a South Asia and Himalaya Search Engine. And links.

http://www.afronet.org.za
A starting point for sites on African culture and ethnicity.

http://www.latinolink.com
Links for Latino awareness sites.

Native American

http://www.religioustolerance.org/nataspir
This site is an excellent example of a site about indigenous cultures. It carries a clear, simple yet profound explanation of Native American spiritual practices and beliefs, which form an integral and seamless part of traditional daily life. It explains where Native Americans originated, their development and history, the diversity of cultural and spiritual traditions, and particular groups such as Inuit and northwest Pacific tribes. Native American contributions to modern life are acknowledged including the first oral contraceptive as well as over 200 drugs that are derived from native remedies. There is a very good introduction to such topics as Inuit Shamanism, Native American deities and creation mythology, cosmology, vision quest and sweat lodges. Plus an excellent set of book references and website links.

http://www.afn.org/~native/
Native American Tribes – links to tribal info, native studies and media issues.

http://www.iwchildren.org
American Comments – a web magazine dealing with aboriginal issues.

http://www.nativeamericanembassy
The Native American Embassy and the Native American Holocaust Museum share this website.

http://www.indians.org
Historical Native American information.

http://www.naturallynative.com
A movie website.

<u>Activism</u>

http://www.urban75.com
A highly recommended UK site, non-profit in orientation. Essentially an alternative e-zine with pages on direct action, raves, drug info, football and 'useless' stuff. It is excellently designed and well written, with amusing little features like the java-enabled 'punch a celebrity' archive.

http://www.newsociety.com

New Society is an 'activist' publisher, chiefly of sustainability and ecological interest titles. Download its catalogue from here, browse new titles, and find your local stockist.

http://www.amnesty.org
http://www.amnesty.at

Still working tirelessly for human rights worldwide.

http://www.greenpeace.org

The ubiquitous and dynamic organization with its activist approach to environmental action. Check out their toxic watch map.

http://www.acgc.org

Action Coalition for Global Change – 'working towards peace, sustainability and equal human rights for all'.

http://www.future.org

Devoted to living in a sustainable and equitable way.

Lifestyle and voluntary simplicity

http://www.simpleliving.net

Tools for those who are serious about downshifting – learning to live a more conscious, simple, healthy and earth-friendly lifestyle. Includes publications.

http://www.fururenet.org
Positive Futures Network. An independent non-profit organization offering positive options in community, healing, economics, technology and sustainability.

http://www.newdream.org
Center for a New American Dream – a not-for-profit organization dedicated to reducing resource consumption and improving the real quality of life.

http://www.seedsofsimplicity.org
A US non-profit membership organization presenting voluntary simplicity as a social and environmental issue to mainstream society.

http://www.newhorizons.org
An influential resource for educational change, which has been implementing educational strategies since 1980.

http://www.newroadmap.org
Provides people with practical tools and innovative approaches for dealing with basic life challenges. Emphasizes service as a means to personal health and social revitalization.

Peacework

http://www.oneworld.net

The extensive and slickly designed One World website is
international in outlook and comprehensive in implementation of its intention to 'harness the democratic power
of the Internet'. Recommended to anyone interested in
current peace issues worldwide.

http://www.people4peace.com

A colourful and basic website that is essentially a collection of links to peace sites and resources. There is an
emphasis on kids' interest links, too.

http://www.kids4peace.com

Another colourful, simple website: a peace site for

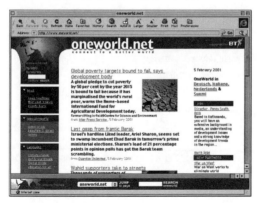

children including stories, 'print-out-and-colour-in' drawings, a play, and more.

http://www.grandmothersforpeace.org
The long established (1982) Grandmothers for Peace organization has its website here. Newsletters, information and activism ideas from this laudable project.

www.peacecorps.gov
The official site of the US Government's Peace Corps initiative. Well designed and informative.

http://www.cybernaute.com
This is the portal site of the Earth Rainbow Network, an umbrella for a host of organizations. The collective goal is to offer the world ways to create a shift of consciousness towards peace, unity and a sustainable relationship with all other life forms. The whole thing grew out of plans for a millennium gathering called Earth Concert 2000, created back in 1997.

http://www.worldpeace2000.com
A comprehensive resource site on peace, with many recommended links such as Action Without Borders, Bookmarks for a Better World, Global Volunteers, and Dr Robert Muller's Ideas and Dreams for a Better World. Plus contacts worldwide.

http://www.pilgrim2.com

The travels, adventures and teachings of the travelling pilgrim for peace. Provides methods for living peacefully and with compassion. Includes an option called '7 constructive ideas per week'.

Women's Movement

http://www.womansource.com

A good site – comprehensive, well designed and functional, and full of links to other good sites covering a whole range of women's issues. As well as its own pages on books, women's groups and events, there is a hotlist of other great sites, some of which are slick and professional, while others are nascent student projects.

http://www.awomansjourney.com

Covers a wide range of spiritual growth and enlightenment topics, from meditation and crystals to Feng Shui and Native American spirituality.

http://www.womensmedia.com

Self-improvement site for women.

http://www.cthonia.com

A 'cyberspace retreat for women', focusing on personal growth and the art of being a woman in mind-body-spirit. No trivia or advertising – it's a promise.

http://www.chickclick.com
A hip web-centred web portal.

http://www.women.com
For women who want to know and do more about their health and fitness, as well as about children and career.

http://www.smith.edu/~aaustin
Amazonian Warrior Chicks for Nicaraguan Feminism. Unfortunately this site does not seem to explain how to become an 'Amazonian Warrior Chick'.

http://www.spunk.org
'Essential anarcho-feminist texts'.

http://www.users.bigpond.com
'Sympathy for the Male' resource for women.

Men's Movement

http://www.castlebooks.com/man.html
A searchable database of 1,500 URLs dedicated to men's issues.

http://www.ncfm.org
The New-York-based National Coalition for Free Men's website is here. Basic in design, it contains a large number of links and resources including an e-zine gazette and an

FTP site from which you can download articles and research.

http://www.menshealth.com
A portal site from the magazine for all male health issues: clear and comprehensive.

http://www.refdesk.com/men.html
A collection of links to a selection of men's interest web-sites.

http://www.malesurvivor.org/
This is a website for male survivors of abuse. Its main feature is a chat room and forum, and it also has a small search engine for men, on abuse survival and related issues.

http://www.mensproject.org
This project is based in Northern Ireland, and aims to address men's concerns there. It is a simple website, with good content, and web links in its resources section.

http://www.psychstat.smsu.edu/mens.htm
Excellent categorized list of resources on all aspects of men's rights.

http://www.penisowner.com/pom/pom.html
Slightly insalubrious site which nevertheless has some interesting technical information for the owner of a penis.

Global consciousness

http://www.newciv.org
This site is about 'exploring emerging new qualities of life on planet Earth'. It's a big site with a lot of different elements. There's a nice quote from the great Margaret Mead: 'Never doubt that a small group of thoughtful, committed citizens can change the world. Indeed, it is the only thing that ever has.'

http://www.monroeinstitute.org
An American organization that aims to promote the evolution of human consciousness and the development of other states of awareness using an audio technology called Hemi-Sync: rather odd, and probably quasi-religious and commercial.

http://www.nas.com/venus
The Venus Project ... 'Redesign of a culture' ...

http://www.anc.or.kr
Academy for New Civilization.

Footnote

'Whatever you believe you can do, or dream you can, begin it. Boldness has genius, power and magic to it.'

Goethe.

28 strange, weird, trivial, funny and rude

Strange and weird

There's a lot of very weird stuff out there. Here's just a little of it.

http://www.onelist.com/subscribe.cgi/hollowearth
Discussion forum mulling over indisputable evidence that the Earth is not, in fact, solid – we only think so, it seems, because the world education system has conspired to have us believe it.

http://www.links.net/www
The Weird, Wild and Wonderful site – a good starting point.

http://www.europa.com/edge/weird
Weird Mysteries Directory of sites involving angels, aliens etc.

http://www.newsoftheweird.com
A collection of strange and amusing stories from the media.

http://www.seti-inst.edu
From the world's top ET-hunters.

http://www.alienabductions.com
Features the 'abductalizer' test.

http://www.jagat.com/joel/socks
Bureau of Missing Socks. Nice one.

http://www.eatbug.com
Insects as food.

http://www.conspire.com
Tongue-in-cheek conspiracy theories and tales.

http://www.disinfo.com
Conspiracies galore.

http://www.forteantimes.com
The ultimate journal of strange phenomena, with lots of authentic pictures.

http://www.QuirkyWorld.com

The weirdest websites and news on what's normal in the world of the abnormal.

http://www.pacificcoast.net./-rick/

Rick believes that his big toe can predict earthquakes that are imminent when it itches.

Trivial and timewasting

http://www.members.spree.com/sci-fi/orion24/ starfleet

Star Fleet astrology info for Star Trek enthusiasts. It's a long address, but trekkies will be meticulous and committed enough to get it right.

http://www.urban75.com/Mag/bubble

Perpetual bubblewrap – shallow but harmless therapy for the stressed-out mind-body-spiriter.

http://www.simeonmagic.com

This one's clever and possibly enlightening. Fun with 'mind magic' that shows you quite a bit about how your mind works.

http://www.iqtest.net/newage

New Age IQ test.

http://www.daterate.com

Dating calculator – calculate your chance of a 'successful' date or encounter each day.

Cute

http://www.thekiss.com

Tales of first ever kisses and best ever kisses.

http://www.virtualchocolate.com

Virtual chocolate gifts.

Rude

http://www.kama-sooty.co.uk

British humour here in a delightful parody of the oriental classic of eroticism. It features the legendary glove puppet Sooty and his friends demonstrating the full range of sexual positions. The term bestiality takes on a whole new meaning. Good clean fun.

http://www.prawnography.net

Another spoof porno site which effectively lampoons its less savoury cousins festooning the Net these days. Experience hardcore prawn and saucy stuff. You'll need Flash and Quicktime to enjoy the best bits.

Funny

http://www.dmoz.org/Religion_and_Spirituality/Humor
Has 54 links of varying quality and funniness. Spiritual comedy can be a serious business.

http://www.aquarianage.org/lore/jokes
Collection of astrological jokes and humour, e.g. how many astrologers does it take to change a light bulb?

Bad

No directory would be complete without some generally agreed examples of bad web design and presentation or taste. Here are a few leads, as voted by Internet magazines.

http://www.webpagesthatsuck.com
Exhibits some stinkers and explains how you can avoid making similar mistakes.

http://www.users2.50megs.com/reptile
The Reptilian Research Archives – serpentine stuff from David Icke.

http://www.airsicknessbags.com
Vomit receptacles from the world's airlines.

http://www.ncf.carleton.ca/~de440

Best hydroponics. One magazine called this the worst looking site they'd ever seen.

And finally ...

http://home.att.net/~cecw/lastpage

The Very Last Page on the Whole Internet.

glossary of internet terms

ADSL Asymmetric Digital Subscriber Line – a method of transmitting digital information over telephones at high bandwidths.

Attachment A file that is transferred along with an email message.

Bandwidth The amount of data that can be transmitted per second – the higher the figure, the faster the transfer.

Bookmarks Websites that a user has marked and recorded for future revisiting.

Bluetooth A new protocol for connecting and delivering information to mobile computing devices.

Broadband A communications medium that can transfer multiple streams of data simultaneously.

Browser A program that connects to and reads web pages.

Cache A temporary store of computer information; specifically, where the browser temporarily stores the webpages most recently visited.

Chat Live conversation with a number of other people over the Internet.

Content Information of interest or value on a webpage, as opposed to advertising or window-dressing.

Cookie A small text file that is placed on a user's computer by a website's server to serve as an identity tag and tracking device.

Cybersquatting Reserving a domain name in order to sell it.

Default A term describing the settings that are adopted by any software application or computer system in the absence of others being substituted by the user.

Domain name Part of a website's URL that identifies the site.

Downloading Loading material such as a web page or software program from the Web onto a user's computer screen or memory.

Email Messages sent electronically from one computer to another, either via the Internet or directly by telephone lines.

Executable files Files that 'do' something when they are opened, often sent as attachments to emails. They are usually identifiable by the prefix 'exe', and are particularly useful for carrying viruses.

Eye candy Eye-catching visual elements of a website's design.

FAQ Frequently Asked Questions on any topic or area of interest.

Firewall Software that protects the contents of computers from unauthorized access.

Flaming Sending inflammatory emails or Usenet messages.

Fluff Uninteresting or irrelevant website content.

FTP File Transfer Protocol – a method of transferring files between computers over the Internet.

GIF Graphic Image File format – a compressed format for transferring graphics on the Internet.

Hacker A person who breaks through computer security systems, and may interfere with their websites.

Hits The number of times a site is visited by surfers; these are usually counted by a hit counter, and the number is often displayed on the site.

Home page The opening page of a website, that introduces the rest. Also the opening page that you choose for your web browser.

html HyperText Markup Language – the universal language of the Web, in which all pages are written.

http HyperText Transfer Protocol – the main text format used on the Web.

IRC Internet Relay Chat – a program that enables real-time discussions on the Internet.

ISDN Integrated Services Digital Network – a method for transferring large amounts of data over telephone lines at high speed.

ISP Internet Service Provider – a company which provides connection to the Net.

JPEG Joint Photographic Experts Group – a highly compressed file format for transferring images via the Web.

Keyword A word that is typed into a search tool to find relevant sites.

Links Underlined words or images that can connect the user directly from one website to another by clicking on them.

Log on To connect to the Internet.

Lurker An online discussion group participant who prefers to read other people's messages rather than posting their own views.

Modem Modulator/Demodulator – a device that connects computers to the Internet via telephone lines.

MP3 A digital format for transferring compressed audio files with high quality.

Newsgroups Discussion groups which are held over the Net, also known as Usenet.

Newsreader Software for reading messages sent to newsgroups.

Offline Not connected to the Internet.

Online Connected to the Internet.

PDA Personal Digital Assistant – a small hand-held computer.

PDF Portable Document Format – a file type that retains document formatting on any computer.

Plug-in A small program that extends the capabilities of a larger program, often downloadable free from the Net.

Portal A website that offers a starting place for surfing to other sites for many users.

Search engine A website that contains search facilities for finding other pages with specific content.

Secure site A site which provides protection for commercial transactions.

Sidebar A separate panel of text or pictures that appears as a supplement to the side of a main web page.

Signature A section of text that an email user can add automatically to any email, for instance to supply contact details or other repetitively required information.

Spam Junk or unsolicited emails, usually posted on a large scale.

Stickiness The quality that leads users to stay at a website.

Streaming Sound or video that can start playing while the remainder downloads.

Surfing Travelling round the Internet, visiting different sites by following links.

Tags Keywords used in a website and supplied to search engines so that the site can be retrieved by surfers who key in those terms in their searches. Also known as metatags.

Uploading Sending information from a user's computer via the Internet.

URL Uniform Resource Locator – the web address of a website or other web resource.

WAP Wireless Application Protocol – a system that enables certain mobile phones and other devices to access specially formatted Internet content.

Web The World Wide Web – part of the Internet where websites are stored and accessed.

Webring A series of thematically connected websites connected in a circular pattern.

index